The task is to build a curriculum that will achieve a set of consistent ideas and values in which all members of society can share. A desirable curriculum is one that reflects a consistent cultural point of view and attempts to achieve a mutual adjustment of cultural elements in terms of a common orientation. An undesirable curriculum, on the other hand, is one that accentuates the maladjustment of cultural elements by stressing those traditional ideals, knowledges, sentiments, and skills no longer relevant to social realities.
—Smith, Stanley, and Shores, pp. 21–22

There are legitimate arguments to be made for a variety of stances on the best goals for schools and students, on the essential curriculum that will lead to those goals, on what the most important characteristics of citizens are, on how much control is too much, and on what kinds of reforms will lead to better educative experiences for kids. We ought to have thought through and clearly articulated a stance on such critical questions.
—Hinchey and Konkol, pp. 194–195

A Coherent Curriculum for Every Student: Curriculum Proposals for Possible Adoption

Edmund C. Short

London • New York

Published by Rowman & Littlefield
An imprint of The Rowman & Littlefield Publishing Group, Inc.
4501 Forbes Boulevard, Suite 200, Lanham, Maryland 20706
www.rowman.com

6 Tinworth Street, London SE11 5AL, United Kingdom

Copyright © 2020 by Edmund C. Short

All rights reserved. No part of this book may be reproduced in any form or by any electronic or mechanical means, including information storage and retrieval systems, without written permission from the publisher, except by a reviewer who may quote passages in a review.

British Library Cataloguing in Publication Information Available

Library of Congress Cataloging-in-Publication Data Available

ISBN 978-1-4758-5260-8 (cloth)
ISBN 978-1-4758-5261-5 (pbk.)
ISBN 978-1-4758-5262-2 (electronic)

Contents

Preface	ix
INTRODUCTION	**1**
The Issue of Curriculum	1
What This Book Contains	2
Why These Curriculum Proposals Are Offered for Your Consideration	5
What Exactly Are Curriculum Proposals?	7
PART I: ACADEMIC-FOCUSED CURRICULUM PROPOSALS	**11**
1 Coherent Proposals with an Academic Focus	13
Adler (1982): Proposal 1	13
Broudy, Smith, Burnett (1964): Proposal 2	15
Chaucer (2012): Proposal 3	17
Egan (1997): Proposal 4	19
Gardner (1999): Proposal 5	21
King, Brownell (1966): Proposal 6	23
Phenix (1964): Proposal 7	25
2 Partial Proposals with an Academic Focus	27
Bennett (1987), Eisner (1982), Gardner (2008), Hirsch (1988), Koerner (1959), Parker, Rubin (1966), Reid (1980)	

PART II: DEMOCRATIC-FOCUSED CURRICULUM PROPOSALS — 31

3 Coherent Proposals with a Democratic Focus — 33
Beane (1997): Proposal 8 — 33
Hopkins (1941): Proposal 9 — 36
White (1991): Proposal 10 — 38

4 Partial Proposals with a Democratic Focus — 40
Banks (2019), Brameld (1945), Educational Policies Commission (1938), Goodlad, Lovitt (1993), Grant (2012), McLaren (2007), Miller (2002), Newmann (1975), Rebell (2018)

PART III: GLOBAL-FOCUSED CURRICULUM PROPOSALS — 43

5 Coherent Proposals with a Global Focus — 45
Goodlad (1974): Proposal 11 — 45
O'Sullivan (1999): Proposal 12 — 47

6 Partial Proposals with a Global Focus — 49
Braus, Wood (1994), Robinson (2015), Santone (2019), Waks (2014)

PART IV: LIVING-FOCUSED CURRICULUM PROPOSALS — 51

7 Coherent Proposals with a Living Focus — 53
James (1972): Proposal 13 — 53
Prensky (2016): Proposal 14 — 57
Stratemeyer, Forkner, McKim, Passow (1947): - Proposal 15 — 60
Totten, Manley (1969): Proposal 16 — 64
Weinstein, Fantini (1970): Proposal 17 — 67

8 Partial Proposals with a Living Focus — 69
Battelle for Kids (2019), Bremer (1975), Federal Security Agency (1951), Ontario DOE (1968), Rubin (1969), Rugg (1936)

PART V: PERSON-FOCUSED CURRICULUM PROPOSALS — 73

9 Coherent Proposals with a Person Focus — 75
Berman (1968): Proposal 18 — 75
Costa, Liebmann (1997): Proposal 19 — 78

	Doll (1993): Proposal 20	80
	Frymier (1973): Proposal 21	82
	Macdonald, Wolfson, Zaret (1973): Proposal 22	85
	Miller (2007): Proposal 23	87
10	Partial Proposals with a Person Focus	89

Barrow (1984), Beane, Lipka (1984), Bookewalter (2003), Cole (1972), Davis (1971), Eble (1966), Ergas (2017), Goodson (2014), Jones, Bouffard (2012), Kilpatrick (1931), Kline (1971), (1968), Leonard Parker (1963), Pinar (1975), Postman, Weingartner (1973), Pritzkau (1971), Rogers (1983), Weiss, Moran, Cottle (1975), Zhoa (2018)

PART VI: PROBLEM-FOCUSED CURRICULUM PROPOSALS — 95

11	Coherent Proposals with a Problem Focus	97
	Collins (2017): Proposal 24	97
	Faunce, Bossing (1958): Proposal 25	100
	Pearl (1972): Proposal 26	103
	Scriven (1972): Proposal 27	104
	Sizer (1992): Proposal 28	106
	Thelen (1972): Proposal 29	109
12	Partial Proposals with a Problem Focus	111

Ammons (1969), Bowers (1974), Hopkins (1994), Marsh, Codding (1999), Miel (1969), Miller (2018), Murname, Levy (1996), Perkins (1986), Raup, Axtelle, Benne, Smith (1962), Swartwood (2013), Wasserman (2018)

PART VII: VALUES-FOCUSED CURRICULUM PROPOSALS — 115

13	Coherent Proposals with a Values Focus	117
	Noddings (1992): Proposal 30	117
	Phenix (1961): Proposal 31	119
	Purpel (1989): Proposal 32	121
	Vandenberg (1990): Proposal 33	123
14	Partial Proposals with a Values Focus	125

Boyer (1995), Egan, Cant, Judson (2013), Frazier (1980), Hantzopoulos (2016), Kimball, McClellan (1962), Miller (2000), Smits, Naqvi (2015), Ulich (1965)

Appendix A: Practical Assistance for Creating a Total Curriculum
    Program from a Curriculum Proposal   129
    Choosing a Viable Curriculum Proposal on Which to Base an
        Actual Curriculum
    Grasping the Place of Curriculum within Historical and
        Contextual Realities
    Finding Guidance on the Curriculum Design Process Itself
    Assuring Coherence in the Curriculum Design and
        Programmatic Features
    References

Appendix B: References Giving What Earlier Curriculum
    Authorities Said Would Be Needed in Future Curricula   145

Appendix C: How to Use This Book   147

About the Author   149

Preface

This book presents a collection of proposals on how school curriculum may be conceived, designed, and realized. These proposals are drawn from writers both past and present who have presented some particular vision of what curriculum could be like for Pre-K–12 schools and have sought to convince others to adopt their proposal for use in actual school situations. The proposals differ from one another in a variety of ways, including in their purposes, their contents, and their perspectives, and thus pose a wealth of options for consideration by those who are planning to change their school curriculum to something new and more suitable for their particular clientele. Readers will need to weigh the appeal of various proposals presented here against criteria they have for locating an optimum model for their particular situation.

The proposals selected for inclusion in this book address the whole of the curriculum—all levels, all subjects, all age groups; they deal with entire program change rather than with incidental changes in content, program arrangements, teaching approaches, or other limited alterations. This book is intended to be a useful resource for those responsible for making decisions in a particular school, school district, or at a broader policymaking level, about what the entire curriculum should be and should include. It draws attention to the work of many thoughtful persons who have dealt with the issue of what a coherent curriculum might be like and who, in some instances, have set up actual programs based on their ideas.

Introduction

THE ISSUE OF CURRICULUM

Curriculum (what it should consist of—what it should be derived from—what it should lead to—and what its role should be in the education of children and youth) is surely a much underdiscussed topic among the powers that be, by the general public, by teachers and other educators, and by parents of students in our schools.

Why is that?

We live in an age when a great many aspects of schooling get a lot of attention in local, state, national, and worldwide debates—matters concerning its governance, its funding, its leadership and staffing, its use of technology and facilities, the challenges presented by its students, their academic achievement or lack thereof, how to teach them and test them, and how to reform the whole system. Yet, seldom do we have serious discussions about what the curriculum in our schools should be like—except perhaps when we don't like what's presently being taught in the local schools we happen to know best. A larger public discussion about what curriculum models might be best for our schools or for our school districts to follow is generally lacking among topics addressed in current educational debates.

Again, why is that?

Perhaps we ignore discussing the curriculum because we think that what it should consist of has already been settled upon by somebody with more expertise on the subject than we have—by the local or state Board of Education, by the state legislature or the U.S. Congress, by the scholars in the disciplines of knowledge, by teachers and curriculum experts, by textbook and test writers, by the proposers of the Common Core State Standards, by corporate or other special interest groups who seem to have the power to get their preferences built into the required curriculum.

Perhaps we ignore discussing the curriculum because we happen to believe the curriculum in place currently is the best possible curriculum and we don't want to change it or argue for something different or better.

Perhaps it's because we don't have any real idea about what's in the current curriculum or don't have any idea about what might be better.

Perhaps it's because we assume that the current curriculum should be the same everywhere for everybody, so if somebody has settled on the one best curriculum for all, why should anyone want to discuss it?

Perhaps it's because we know that the curriculum should be revised and updated but we know how difficult it would be to get people to discuss possible changes and to get them to agree on anything, so we become discouraged or cynical about whether the task could ever be accomplished and we let the whole matter slide and it never gets addressed.

This book aims to convince you that it's possible, even quite necessary, to undertake a public discussion about what would make up a desirable curriculum beyond that which currently exists. It aims to entice you into wanting to discuss matters of curriculum for the sake of our children and youth as if the most pressing question among the whole range of educational issues up for debate is the nature and content of the curriculum. It offers a vast array of ideas to consider in undertaking curriculum revision so that you need not feel at a loss for good ideas to propose and/or adopt.

WHAT THIS BOOK CONTAINS

There are plenty of possible models from the past and the present that you might not have known about and they are gathered here in this book in a summary form for your convenience and for your consideration. You are invited to examine them as a citizen or as an educator whenever curriculum matters come up for discussion and to deliberate about whether any of the many proposed conceptions of curriculum appeal to you for good and solid reasons for your school or school system.

Each of the proposed curriculum models presented here reflects different purposes, content, and outcomes based on varied beliefs and assumptions about what makes up a good educational program in the view of its author. You will find some of them quite compelling in their vision and in their actual programming. You will not see some as viable options because of fundamental disagreements you may have with their underlying assumptions or their practical implications. You should not assume that I endorse any one or all of these proposed curriculum models just because I have brought them to your attention; I have presented them in all their variety because some people somewhere may find themselves in agreement with them and want to argue for their adoption, and because they are substantially well presented and argued for. All of these proposals are meant to embrace the whole of the curriculum rather than just part of it or only some level of schooling or only some subject field or topic.

The proposals presented in this book are divided into seven groups according to a common focus they each exhibit. Part I includes Academic-Focused Proposals, Part II. Democratic-Focused Proposals, Part III. Global-Focused Proposals, Part IV. Living-Focused Proposals, Part V. Person-Focused Proposal, Part VI. Problem-Focused Proposals, and Part VII. Values-Focused Proposals. In each group, I have included a series of Coherent Proposals and a set of Partial Proposals. For the Coherent Proposals I have summarized the ideas presented by each author under a set of common features that I consider any complete curriculum proposal must include. (See my treatment of these features later in this Introduction.) I have also included in each group some additional proposals that are only partially complete but which could no doubt be expanded into complete proposals by someone interested in doing so. I have only briefly annotated these partial curriculum proposals.

This whole array of past and present curriculum proposals that are collected here in an outline form are certainly not the only ones available in the literature. Nor do they preclude the possibility that other new proposals can be created by others with yet different ideas about what curriculum should be like. I have gathered in this single resource the ones I happen to know about from my many years of experience as a student of curriculum, as a curriculum consultant, and as a professor of curriculum. My reason for including the ones appearing here is that I know how few people study the literature of curriculum and are aware of the many excellent options that have been proposed by knowledgeable people with a view to ensuring the welfare of our children and youth. These options need to become more widely known and should not be overlooked. This book should assist in achieving that goal.

As you will see, there is no shortage of ideas available to be considered if people really want to make wise judgments about what they think might be a really good curriculum for any given situation. And because every kind of curriculum model has different consequences for how our children and youth will turn out as persons, citizens, workers, parents, etc., our choice of curriculum is crucial and a heavy responsibility. We need to deliberate carefully among various curriculum options in order to determine what is truly best for our students to pursue throughout their entire school careers. Thus, these curriculum proposals are conveniently summarized in this book for your careful study and action.

Appendix A of this book is a brief primer on how a curriculum proposal, once chosen, can be translated into an actual curriculum program for use in a particular educational setting. If those charged with accomplishing this task do not have the necessary knowledge or expertise to put together an entire curriculum based on one of these proposals, here they will find a kind of short course on this process. It covers what is generally called "curriculum designing" and refers readers to technical advice on this matter as it has been developed over the years by specialists in curriculum planning. While the treatment is not comprehensive in character, it points to helpful resources needed for developing, planning, and implementing whatever curriculum model someone might wish to introduce.

Appendix B contains a list of publications in which curriculum authorities over the last century projected (at the time they were written) what changes in curriculum they thought would be needed in the future. These glimpses ahead are very interesting for us to take note of today—not only for the substantive insights they offered but also for how they make us aware of how few of their projections have been incorporated into our curricula over time. They remind us that even small or incremental revisions in curriculum, to say nothing of overall coherent curriculum revision, have been difficult to achieve. The work of keeping the school curriculum well-conceived and contemporaneously suitable for educating the younger generation is never easy and a never-ending task.

Appendix C provides a series of recommendations on how to use this book for study and action. It suggests steps to take in utilizing this resource as an aid in choosing or finding a preferred curriculum proposal and in deciding to create and plan for an actual curricular program based on that choice.

It may well be the case that we are now in a period of time in the United States, and perhaps elsewhere, when we are freer than we have been for some time to try to improve upon the curricula that we offer in our schools. The restraints are being lifted. Activists in education and in curriculum are beginning to push against whatever restraints still exist and are initiating changes in curriculum that they have wished to make for a long time, but felt they couldn't, given the educational climate and the neoliberal ideology to conform to undesirable norms that has existed for over three decades. Local school authorities, teachers, and curriculum specialists can perhaps once again take charge of making curriculum decisions for their schools in a way that hasn't been possible for quite a while. So, the time may be ripe for us to look again at what kind of curriculum would be most desirable in our various settings and to take the opportunity to choose something more nearly in keeping with our visions of what a good education should be like than what we may have in place right now. This book of curriculum proposals is a good place to start as we begin to rethink our schools' curriculum programs and try to find something more compelling to implement for the education of our children and youth.

WHY THESE CURRICULUM PROPOSALS ARE OFFERED FOR YOUR CONSIDERATION

There are several prominent reasons why this particular set of curriculum models is featured in this book.

First of all, I have tried to identify the proposals that support the assumption held by scholars of curriculum practice: that *any viable curriculum design must have coherence and integrity from beginning to end.* That is, from the earliest age of entry into an organized program of education until the ultimate completion of that program, for example, Pre-K to 12.

In the past, too much of the curriculum that has been planned and implemented has been developed in chunks or segments that do not relate in any explicit way to one another and often confuse both students and teachers as to why they are included or why they follow one another. This is because they were thought of and designed separately and not as a whole package. Whatever integrity or coherence may be present in them is found not by examining the curriculum as a whole but is evident only in the individual segments, such as the science component, or the eighth grade program, or the curriculum for college-goers, or the program for a special-needs group, or a project on social-emotional learning. How does a student who is in all these components of the curriculum at some time between entry into schooling and graduation make sense of these separate pieces if there is no evident coherence or integrity between and among them? The only way to be able to assure that the curriculum as a whole has been designed to have coherence and integrity is to plan it all together as an entire project rather than segment by segment.

All of the curriculum proposals presented in this book have the potential to be models for the whole of a curriculum, not for just parts of it, and offer justifications for their use in designing a curriculum that can be said to have coherence and integrity throughout.

Second, I have tried to identify curriculum proposals that support another assumption held by scholars of curriculum practice: that the way to attain the desired coherence and integrity throughout the entire program is to *adhere to a single unifying idea or concept that is inherent in every phase of the curriculum program from beginning to end.* Does that sound impossible? Have you ever seen a curriculum where such a thread could be seen running through the curriculum from Pre-K to 12?

Sometimes it is evident in an overarching purpose, such as academic excellence. Sometimes it is evident in a particular all-pervasive objective, such as preparation for democratic citizenship. Sometimes it is evident in an ideal of the good life, such as altruism, service to others, or a loving heart. Sometimes it is evident in a set of dispositions or life skills, such as mastery of self-direction or the processes associated with achieving success with the tasks everyone faces at various stages of life. Sometimes it is evident in something as narrow as economic proficiency.

Granted, the task of bringing unity to something as extensive as twelve to fourteen years of schooling is a daunting one. Yet, I argue that it can be achieved, by conceptualizing a single, broadly applicable idea to which every particular goal, subject matter, and curricular feature of the entire curriculum can contribute, thus gaining the desired coherence and integrity. In fact, some would say that using this strategy of establishing a unifying theme, objective, or ideal can actually cut out redundancy and many unnecessary elements of the curriculum that often take up time and energy that could be devoted to matters of more central concern to the overall purposes of the curriculum as dictated by the single unifying idea. It also forces a choice among what possible ideas are to be considered as utmost priority. After all, any curriculum cannot do everything that might be desirable. This principle of curriculum unity can certainly help bring focus and clarity to the curriculum and make it simpler to explain and justify.

Third, I have tried to identify curriculum proposals that support yet another assumption held by scholars of curriculum practice: that while every curriculum should exhibit coherence, integrity, and unity, *every student does not have to have the same curriculum*. All the proposals featured in this volume, while they may set forth particular programmatic specifications consistent with their unique focus and objective, are not dogmatic about being implemented the same way for all students. (Well, some of them may seem like they are, but I contend that several versions of their models can be designed to fit the needs of various students without departing from the basic thrust of the proposals presented.) Indeed, most of them expect to be implemented differentially for different students.

Why is this desirable? Requiring that a curriculum be implemented with the same fidelity to the original model with students who differ so much in timing of their learning, in the pace of their learning, in their development and ability to learn, in the point at which their interest in some aspects of the learning peaks, and in the impact their personal and social lives have on their learning, is just not realistic or feasible. It is far more reasonable to follow a practice of providing a coherent, unified curriculum for each student than it is to impose the same curriculum on all students.

Admittedly, this is tougher to do than to provide a single curriculum for everybody or to provide two or three or even four separate tracks for different groups of students. But it can be done with close and continuous oversight throughout the many years of schooling. And planning for and designing individual curricula for all students is possible within the frameworks presented by the curriculum proposals included in this book.

I have identified thirty-three curriculum proposals that meet the basic assumptions just discussed. Each of these thirty-three curriculum proposals is described in some detail and placed within one of seven categories by its primary focus. Besides the thirty-three fully coherent curriculum proposals featured in this book, I have also included and briefly annotated a large number of partial proposals that also appear within the same set of categories. These partial proposals are missing some element(s) of a complete proposal but contain a key idea and enough about their vision of a new curriculum that it may be possible to conceive and lay out a fuller, more coherent proposal based on them if an effort were made to do so. It, therefore, seems advisable to bring these partial proposals to your attention as well for study and consideration.

WHAT EXACTLY ARE CURRICULUM PROPOSALS?

The purpose of this book is to call attention to past and present proposals for school curriculum that merit consideration or reconsideration, analysis or reanalysis, evaluation or reevaluation, and perhaps adoption or readoption for the next generation of children and youth.

So what is a curriculum proposal?

First of all, a *curriculum proposal is a special kind of document* (among many others that are familiar to those dealing with curriculum development, planning, implementation, and evaluation, such as the official curriculum, curriculum guides, scope and sequence charts, lists of curriculum resources, curriculum standards, assessment plans and tests, curriculum revision schedules, curriculum maps, curriculum reviews, and official curriculum evaluations).

A curriculum proposal is a specific kind of curriculum document that *presents a well-thought-out scheme for what is envisioned as a viable, desirable, and practical curriculum* that has not previously been spelled out in just this form and content. It is intended to be innovative if not deliberatively reformative. (Sometimes broader educational reform proposals contain mandates for curriculum reforms, but they are usually not fully developed in the format of an authentic curriculum proposal, which has to include certain structural elements and arguments and has to meet certain specific criteria in order to qualify technically as a curriculum proposal.)

Second, as just suggested, to be a useful, complete curriculum proposal, *it must contain or treat a series of curricular topics or elements*. Statements should be included that, at minimum, address the following components:

1. *A focal idea* around which the entire proposal is shaped and governed,
2. *A unique objective or a set of unique objectives or goals* implied by this focal idea that the curriculum should fulfill by the time a student has completed or graduated from the curriculum,

3. *A general plan for how the proposed curricular program should be organized* in terms that identify the ways the program is to be matriculated by the student at the various stages and levels of schooling (so that the proposal's focus and unique objectives are embodied in a time, sequence, and content structure),
4. *A general picture of the subject matter to be addressed* within every phase and level of the program organization,
5. *The specific teaching methods and materials required to enact the proposed curriculum*, especially any approaches that may be uniquely required by the nature of the particular proposal,
6. *How the overall proposed curricular program should be evaluated* with respect to whether it has been enacted as proposed and has reached its unique objectives as proposed. (Student assessment ideas are normally addressed within component #5 rather than within component # 6, although they may play a part in overall program evaluation), and, last but not least,
7. *Persuasive arguments for why one should accept each and every facet of the proposed curriculum* and be willing to adopt and implement the proposal. This is a very significant part of any curriculum proposal. Simply recommending something is not enough to justify the proposed program and all its elements, especially if the proposal deviates significantly from what is the usual norm for curricula with which the reader is familiar. This justification component of a curriculum proposal is what ties everything together in a reasoned and unified way, such that the reader can grasp how the vision put forth and the programmatic specifications outlined for it are to be conceived, articulated, and integrated. If the arguments for any or all of these matters are weak or unpersuasive, the reader is unlikely to move ahead to truly wish to accept it or to decide to put it into action.

I use these components as rubrics for my sketches of the thirty-three complete proposals that form the primary content of this book. For each of them, I give a short précis of what the author states regarding each of these components and try to lead the reader to see the vision of the proposed curriculum that the writer presents. I give just enough to whet your appetite for studying the original proposal published by the author if you are intrigued enough by it to want to pursue it in detail. I have included in some cases certain references under the additional heading of *Commentaries/Reviews/Critiques* that you will find helpful in grasping or assessing that particular curriculum proposal. Please note that these rubrics are not followed for the partial curriculum proposals for the obvious reason that they do not include information on all seven of these components.

Third, *a curriculum proposal meets certain normative criteria* that qualify it as an authentic curriculum proposal worthy of serious consideration by those who wish to scout around for new ways to conceive of a desirable curriculum program. The following norms capture these criteria: (1) coherent and consistent, (2) total and whole, (3) complete and full, (4) unified and integral, (5) feasible and doable, (6) justifiable and compelling.

Criterion 1 (coherent and consistent) refers to the presence of a thread of an idea, purpose, or objective that can be detected throughout the entire proposal, which is meant to keep the focus clear and to provide the means by which one can determine whether any aspect of the proposal complies with or deviates from that focus. If it does, it is consistent and coherent throughout, as it should be. If it does not, something has to be changed to make it match criterion 1.

Criterion 2 (total and whole) refers to whether the proposal contains all seven of the required components listed above. If it does, it qualifies as total and whole. If it does not, the missing components will have to be added.

Criterion 3 (complete and full) refers to whether the proposal intends to embrace the entire scope of the curriculum program from K-12 or from entry to graduation. If it does, it qualifies as complete and full. If it does not, if it treats only certain grade levels, or certain subject areas, or certain levels of schooling (early childhood, elementary, junior high, or senior high), or certain groups of students (college prep, special education), then it is incomplete and needs to be expanded to cover the full range of time, levels, and students.

Criterion 4 refers to the ideal of having all aspects of the curriculum program governed by the principles, assumptions, and values set forth in the proposal (unified and integral) on the basis of which the entire program is built. If one can find no aspect of the proposal that is not truly based on these principles, assumptions, and values, then it qualifies as unified and integral. If, on the other hand, some aspect seems to violate these principles, assumptions, and values, it does not qualify as unified and integral and these aspects must be excised from the proposal and other matters included that will make it qualify as meeting criterion 4. Most often, treatment of this norm is dealt with in connection with whatever attempts are made to justify and argue for the worth of the proposal (component 7).

Criterion 5 (feasible and doable) refers to the attention given to the practicality of the proposed curriculum program. If the proposal appears to be so utopian that it unlikely to be implementable, then it does not qualify as feasible or doable. If attention is given in the proposal to matters bearing on feasibility or practicality, then it meets criterion 5. Why propose a new curriculum if it is unrealistic in any of its features? A curriculum proposal is not a document of literary fiction; it is a document meant to be feasible and implementable in the real world.

Criterion 6 refers to the quality of the proposal's arguments (justifiable and compelling). Judging how compelling the arguments are throughout every aspect of the proposal as they are presented is what is referred to in criterion 6, not just that arguments have been given. Some proposals may be so scantily argued for or so unpersuasively argued for that one could not conclude that they meet criterion 6. If they do seem to include justifiable and compelling arguments, however, they will meet criterion 6. As would be expected, proposals that overwhelmingly meet this criterion are ones that are mostly likely to be picked up and put into practice.

In case it isn't clear from reading this section on the normative criteria for an authentic curriculum proposal, I should point out that a viable curriculum proposal must meet all six criteria.

A few words are in order concerning who writes curriculum proposals. Most of those I have chosen to highlight here were written by people who have spent a lot of time dealing with curriculum issues, theories, and practices, and have come forth with ideas that struck them as being better than ones they saw in operation in schools with which they were familiar. (Some actually created schools that eventually generated curricula that they wished to propose for others to follow.) Many of these were curriculum scholars, but also many were school leaders and curriculum specialists working in school settings. Some of those who wrote partial proposals also came from these same domains while others had less connection with curriculum work per se but were able to generate some interesting ideas worthy of study.

Anyone presumably can create a curriculum proposal, and I suggest that you try to do so yourself, especially if after reading all the proposals in this book you find none of them particularly appealing. You should, however, try to take into account what I have presented here about the nature of such proposals and try to include all the formal components mentioned and try to meet all the stated criteria.

Part I

ACADEMIC-FOCUSED CURRICULUM PROPOSALS

1

Coherent Proposals with an Academic Focus

PROPOSAL 1

Adler, Mortimer J., *The Paideia Proposal: An Educational Manifesto.* New York: Macmillan Publishing Company, 1982. 84 pp.

Adler, Mortimer J., *Paideia Problems and Possibilities.* New York: Macmillan Publishing Company, 1983. 113 pp.

Adler, Mortimer J., *The Paideia Program: An Educational Syllabus.* New York: Macmillan Publishing Company, 1984. 238 pp.

Focus: Proposes the same basic, general, nonspecialized, academic schooling for all students (no tracks).

Unique Objective: To attain a three-pronged general education that includes: (1) personal growth or self-improvement—mental, moral and spiritual, (2) cultivation of civic virtues and knowledge of government that enfranchises one as a citizen of the republic, and (3) preparation for earning a living in one occupation or another. In other words, to lead intelligent and responsible lives as persons, citizens, and workers.

Program Organization: The proposed curriculum (required of all students) is to be organized into three branches as follows: (1) Acquisition of Knowledge, (2) Development of Intellectual Skills, and (3) Enlarged Understanding of Ideas and Values. All three branches are to be studied for the full twelve years of schooling. Auxiliary subjects such as physical education, manual arts, and induction into the world of work are required in shorter than twelve-year spans.

Selection of Content: The branch devoted to Acquisition of Knowledge would include language, literature, fine arts, mathematics, natural sciences, history, geography, and social studies. The branch devoted to Intellectual

Skills would include reading, writing, speaking, listening, calculating, problem-solving, observing, measuring, estimating, and exercising critical judgment. The branch devoted to Ideas and Values would include discussion of great books and works of art, involvement in artistic activities such as music, drama, and the visual arts. The author notes that this description of the content of the three branches does not imply separate courses within each branch; courses could cross branches.

Teaching Methods and Materials: Didactic instruction, lectures and responses, textbooks, and other aids would be used in teaching first branch objectives. Coaching, exercises, and supervised practice would be used in teaching second branch objectives. Maieutic or Socratic questioning and active participation in seminars would be used in teaching third branch objectives.

The proposed model program is not meant to be adopted uniformly everywhere. Particular courses, units, and materials of instruction would be chosen for each level of schooling for each local situation according to local circumstances and student needs. However, the proposal does insist on including the three branches, the three modes of learning, and the three modes of teaching. Especially highlighted is the intellectual character of the program and the value and importance of the third branch and its use of Socratic methods.

The 1982 book presents a brief outline of this proposal and the basic argument for its use. The 1983 and 1984 books provide a wide array of illustrative examples of possible questions teachers might have about this proposal as well as examples of possible subjects, courses, activities, methods of implementation, and readings that might fit with the proposed program.

Program Evaluation: Little attention is given to overall program evaluation.

Commentaries/Reviews/Critiques: The 1983 book lists in Appendix One a number of reviews in newspapers and magazines. Appendix Two gives reports of school districts that adopted this proposal.

James E. Isaacs, *Contemporary Education,* 54(Summer, 1983), 314–315.
A Symposium, *Harvard Educational Review,* 53(December, 1983), 377–411.
Nel Noddings, *Journal of Thought,* 19(Spring, 1984), 81–91.
Joseph Watras, Chapter 12 in Joseph L. DeVitis, ed., *Popular Educational Classics: A Reader.* New York: Peter Lang, 2016.

PROPOSAL 2

Broudy, Harry S., B. Othanel Smith, and Joe R. Burnett. *Democracy and Excellence in American Secondary Education.* Chicago, IL: Rand McNally, 1964; Huntington, NY: Robert E. Krieger Publishing Company, 1978. 302 pp.

Focus: A common curriculum for general education for all students

Unique Objective: To build cognitive, evaluative, and interpretive maps of content in five broad areas of study

Program Organization: Symbolic Skills, Basic Science Concepts, Developmental Studies, Value Exemplars, Molar or Social Problems

Selection of Content: This proposal calls for the five areas of study to run from K–12 (but primarily discussed for secondary school), for content to be selected primarily on the basis of interpretive use of knowledge, for content selection to be left to subject matter specialists, for content to be arranged in appropriate sequences for learning, for the same units of content to be taught at three levels to accommodate student differences, and for students to be ungraded and to move up from level three to level two to level one through all units of content as soon as they are able.

Symbolic Skills consist of language skills of reading, writing, speaking, and mathematics; artistic skills; bodily skills; and industrial arts skills.

Basic Science Concepts consist of disciplinary concepts in language, mathematics, general science, biology, chemistry, physics, economics, and other social sciences.

Developmental Studies consist of historical development of the cosmos, of institutions, and of culture.

Value Exemplars consist of the norms embodied in exemplars from the arts, literature, philosophy, and religion. The tasks here are to learn to distinguish between personal taste and intrinsic value, and to develop enduring evaluative maps of appreciation through study of exemplary works.

Molar or Social Problems consist of engagement with problems of general life predicaments and issues of society and citizenship. They involve experiential learning to use integrative knowledge and problem-solving strategies to reach a course of action for oneself or in a group or civic body.

Teaching Methods and Materials: Each area of study has its own unique teaching methods as appropriate to the nature of its units of study. Examples are given throughout the discussion of each. Perhaps the area of Value Exemplars requires methods not commonly known (as they are for the other categories of study). It may consist of study of a relatively few exemplars to acquire aesthetic judgment by means of one's response to the sensuous elements of the work, the formal qualities (form or design) of the work, the technical merits of the work, and the expressive significance or meaning of the work.

Program Evaluation: Very little is stated on this topic.

Commentaries/Reviews/Critiques:

Sidney Rosen, *Journal of Research in Science Teaching*, 2(No. 2, 1964), 163.

C. Arnold Anderson, *Studies in Philosophy and Education*, 4(March, 1965), 6–14.

PROPOSAL 3

Chaucer, Harry, *The DaVinci Curriculum: A Creative Approach to the Common Core Standards*. Lanham, MD: Rowman & Littlefield Publishers, 2012. 208 pp.

Focus: A liberal arts curriculum for Grades 7–12 that is rooted in the history of ideas and is designed to achieve the high standards of the Common Core State Standards of 2010.

Unique Objective: To study our common species and human culture through personalized and meaningful engagement with intellectually rich ideas and activities from all the arts and sciences and guided by commonly accepted standards so that students become insightful and ethical persons and citizens of a democracy.

Program Organization: This proposal is organized by historical periods: Creation—from the Origin of the Universe to 10000 BCE (for Grade 7); Into Civilization—from 10000 BCE to 200 CE (for Grade 8); Age of Faith—from 200 CE to 1400 CE (for Grade 9); Encounter and Change—from 1400 to 1700 (for Grade 10); Rise of Liberalism, Industrialism, and Globalization—from 1700 to 1900 (for Grade 11), and Twentieth and Twenty-First Centuries (for Grade 12). The rationale for this structure rests partly on the liberal arts tradition and partly on the broad sweep of the life and contributions of Leonardo DaVinci, the inspiration for this proposal and for its name.

The author indicates that some other broadly educated person could possibly be taken as a model and inspiration for a similar type of liberal arts curriculum (for which the same structure as prescribed for the DaVinci Curriculum—historical periods might be used). It happens to be named the DaVinci Curriculum because of the choice made by a school that created and implemented it with which the author was affiliated (The Gailer School).

The book suggests topics or themes that might be used within the above-specified periods around which subdivisions of each grade-level year could be organized.

The proposal states that the DaVinci Curriculum is only part of a total program. There are satellite programs to be made available in areas such as mathematics, languages, service learning, fitness and sports, and various forms of inquiry.

Selection of Content: The topics or themes chosen locally would be addressed with multidisciplinary content. Many examples, both suggested and some reported from use in the aforementioned DaVinci Curriculum school, are to be found throughout this book. For example, a unit on Evolution lists readings and activities from historical or scientific texts, science investigations, short stories and other literary texts, geography, religion, performing arts, visual and musical arts, and mathematics—all disciplines that may be appropriate to the topic.

Teaching Methods and Materials: Teachers are to assist students in selection and use of topics and approaches to achieve the goals of the curriculum. Since it is basically a humanistic curriculum, teachers must enable students to personalize their learning. They must provide a high quality of experience for students rather than a high quantity of knowledge. Nevertheless, teachers need to be able to prepare their students in the fundamentals of the disciplines as they apply to the topics and grade levels at which they are working. Teachers must be able to identify content from the various disciplines that can be utilized with topics at their students' grade levels. Also, they must assure that the lessons, their rigor, and their outcomes enable students to meet the Common Core State Standards. Some guidance for teachers appears throughout the book. The assumption is that teachers will have knowledge and skills in all of these areas sufficient for their tasks. Nothing much is said about teacher assignments to grade levels or content fields; implied is the fact that they must be widely prepared in a wide range of disciplines at least at the grade levels and for the topics dealt with at those levels. Consequently, this curriculum is very demanding, not only for students, but also for teachers.

Program Evaluation: One page is devoted to this topic; no unique suggestions are made.

Commentaries/Reviews/Critiques:
https://en.wikipedia.org/wiki/The_Gailer_School
https://rowman.com/ISBN/9781610486729

Please note: Many schools exist that have the name DaVinci. Most are not related to the curriculum model presented in this proposal.

PROPOSAL 4

Egan, Kieran, *The Educated Mind: How Cognitive Tools Shape Our Understanding.* Chicago, IL: The University of Chicago Press, 1997. 299 pp.

Focus: A single-focused coherent curriculum that overcomes contradictions in achieving the conventional three-pronged purposes of socialization, acquiring of knowledge and truth, and fostering of individual potential.

Unique Objective: To acquire five kinds of understanding by learning to use the cognitive/intellectual tools appropriate to each of these. The five kinds of understanding are identified as follows: (1) Somatic Understanding, (2) Mythic Understanding, (3) Romantic Understanding, (4) Philosophic Understanding, and (5) Ironic Understanding. The author provides an extensive treatment of each of these forms of understanding, with cultural and historical examples/rationales from the early Greeks down to current times. This proposal is based on stages of development of cognitive tools that are shared by all human beings and not on stages of growth and maturity.

Program Organization: This proposal contains more of a curriculum framework than a definite program organization. Local curriculum planners can design their own program organization consistent with the proposed objective and framework.

The framework is based on a theory of cognitive development that the author describes in full detail. Humans initially have a "pre-language consciousness" that provides "somatic understanding." At the next stage we develop speech and participate in oral exchanges using narratives, fantasy, metaphor, rhythm and rhyme, images, jokes, abstractions, binary thinking, and story structures—"mythic understanding." Next we enter a stage of "romantic understanding" where we learn to use alphabetic script for writing and reading. Here we are attracted to forms of rationality and reality through tales of heroic bravery, great historic events, the unfamiliar, wonder and awe, the transcendent, etc. The stage of "philosophic understanding" follows thereafter with the development of systematic theoretic thinking. Philosophic thinking generates the capacity to see general schemes and truths, patterns, recurrences, processes, essences, and ordering principles and theories, even uncertainties and anomalies, in the world of nature and ideas. The stage of "ironic understanding" is characterized by nonliteral forms of language, skepticism vs belief, reflectiveness upon ideas vs reality, making problematic what was not previously considered problematic, and thinking about the ethical, aesthetic, and intellectual dimensions of our lives and world.

The author makes the point that, while there is a definite age sequence to these developmental stages (from 1 to 5), each new stage does not develop to the exclusion of the preceding stages. These are not discrete stages; each new stage incorporates all of the preceding stages as they develop. For instance, even at the stages of philosophic and ironic understanding, elements of somatic, mythic, and romantic understanding are present.

Selection of Content: Here, too, content selection is expected to be accomplished by teachers and others at the local level. At each level of schooling, from childhood, through adolescence, to high school and college, subject matter should be chosen that is appropriate for the matching stage of understanding stipulated in the theory of cognitive development. This proposal includes illustrations of appropriate content for each stage from disciplines such as history, language and literature, science, mathematics, rhetoric, and others; however, it does not outline a prescribed set of content for each of the five stages of understanding. Even illustrative themes are suggested in some cases. The book gives less help for choosing content for somatic and ironic understanding than for the other three kinds. School settings where this type of curriculum has been created are also mentioned.

Teaching Methods and Materials: To develop each of the five kinds of understanding, somewhat different materials and teaching methods need to be employed. Since, at all stages beyond the first one, there is a mix of stages, there is room for interdisciplinary approaches, such as individual or group projects.

Play and physical activity are key to developing *somatic understanding* for infants. Telling stories to children from preschool to about age eight is most fitting for the development of *mythic understanding*. Organizing a lesson on the properties of air, for instance, or on a famous scientist, into story form are examples given of methods appropriate for this stage. *Romantic understanding*, introduced from ages eight to fifteen, calls for learning to use written language, including both the technical aspects of writing and reading, and also the grasping of concepts in written or visual form from many fields of subject matter. *Philosophic understanding* requires that a topic (such as the Industrial Revolution) be organized around some general scheme (such as the liberal/progressive meta-narrative) within which the details of the Industrial Revolution can be explored. A helpful discussion of how these five understandings can be taught appears in this proposal, less on ironic than on the others. How a student's learning can be assessed is also to be found here.

Program Evaluation: This topic is not addressed in this proposal.

Commentaries/Reviews/Critiques:
http://www.educ.sfu.ca/kegan/EdMind.html (Several Reviews)
Kieran Egan, *The Future of Education: Reimagining American Schools from the Ground Up*. New Haven, CT: Yale University Press, 2008.
Kieran Egan, with Bob Dunton and Gillian Judson, *Whole School Projects: Engaging Imaginations through Interdisciplinary Inquiry*. New York: Teachers College Press, 2014.

PROPOSAL 5

Gardner, Howard, *The Disciplined Mind: What All Students Should Understand*. New York: Simon & Schuster, 1999. 287 pp.

Focus: A virtue filled understanding of the disciplines focused on the true, the beautiful, and the good in a set of key human achievements

Unique Objective: "World citizens that are highly literate, disciplined, capable of thinking critically and creatively, knowledgeable about a range of cultures, able to participate actively in discussions about new discoveries and choices, and willing to take risks for what they believe in." This vision intends "to transmit roles, to convey cultural values, to inculcate literacies, and to communicate certain disciplinary content and ways of thinking." This proposal contains lengthy elaborations on each of the features mentioned.

Program Organization: The overall structure of this proposal is merely suggested rather than specified. It is conveyed largely by giving illustrative examples of possible ways of organizing this educational program and by calling for local rather than centralized authorities to make these decisions.

Generally, the pattern that is suggested falls into three categories of the disciplines: the sciences, the arts, and history. Within each, a set of human achievements is to be studied that will enhance students' deep understanding of truth (and falsity), beauty (and ugliness), goodness (and evil) as defined by their cultures. The illustrative examples the author provides are: (1) Darwin and evolution (in the case of science/the realm of truth); (2) Mozart and his music, *The Marriage of Figaro* (in the case of the arts/the realm of beauty); and the Holocaust (in the case of history/the realm of morality).

While this proposal stresses organizing by disciplinary categories, the author recognizes that other patterns may also be appropriate for some students in a given setting. Six possible pathways are recommended for each setting so that all children can be accommodated and student and cultural preferences can be met: (1) the canon pathway, (2) the multicultural pathway, (3) the progressive pathway, (4) the technological pathway, (5) the socially responsible pathway, and (6) the understanding pathway (the book focuses on this one and is personally preferred by the author, but all pathways are briefly described). The program's purposes remain the same for all six pathways.

Selection of Content: Within the organizational parameters stated above, content selection at various stages of education is the task of teachers and local officials. Many different options are expected to be evident in the content selected given student and cultural differences. A broad principle should guide the selection of content: one or a few topics should be specified in each category or level of education; no exhaustive coverage of disciplinary content is to be attempted. What is to be grasped by students is the way the topic exemplifies the virtues of truth, beauty, and goodness (or their opposites). In-depth specialization comes, by implication, at some other stage of education. The curriculum proposed in this book is for *all* students. Several exemplary schools are cited which presently incorporate some or most of the vision described herein.

Teaching Methods and Materials: Considerable attention to teaching and teaching methods is to be found in this proposal, much of which is based on the author's research on multiple intelligences and other psychological questions. He also provides several practical criteria for choosing teaching methods and materials. These include providing powerful entry points (several are mentioned), offering apt analogies, and providing multiple representations of the core ideas of the topic, all of which are described with examples. Teachers are free to employ approaches that they find appropriate in their circumstances. Assessment methods fall under the same rationale, but excessive standardized testing is deemed inappropriate under this model.

Program Evaluation: Treatment of this topic is limited. The proposal's objectives, however, give a good idea of what measures and standards would be included in an overall program evaluation.

Commentaries/Reviews/Critiques:

Mary Eberstadt, *Policy Review,* 97(October/November, 1999), 3–17.

Alison Gopnik, *New York Review of Books,* 46(1999), 33–35.

Decker F. Walker, *Fundamentals of Curriculum*, 2nd ed. Mahwah, NJ: Lawrence Erlbaum, 2003. See pp. 79–92.

Veronica Boix Mansilla and Howard Gardner, *Educational Leadership*, 65(February, 2008), 14–19.

PROPOSAL 6

King, Arthur R., Jr., and John A. Brownell, *The Curriculum and the Disciplines of Knowledge: A Theory of Curriculum Practice*. New York: John Wiley & Sons, 1966; Huntington, NY: Robert E. Krieger Publishing Company, 1976. 221 pp.

Focus: The intellect has the prime claim on the curriculum. "Every student is worthy of an encounter with the disciplines of knowledge."

Unique Objective: Though the human being has the need for education in a variety of areas (based on the claims of occupational life, of political life, of social life, of religious life, and of intellectual life), schooling (through its organized curriculum) should be limited to addressing the claims of the intellectual life. The other claims are to be addressed outside of formal schooling by other institutions or through informal learning.

Program Organization: The disciplined structures of knowledge are to constitute the scope and organization of the curriculum. These structures of knowledge provide the human mind with symbolic content useful for reasoning, imagining, making reality intelligible, facing new situations, seeking truth, and controlling one's acts with ethical considerations—amid human striving for freedom, duty, honor, mercy, and love. Human beings are essentially symbolizers. Within this view, the curriculum is to be organized around the separate disciplines of knowledge.

Selection of Content: Though every stage of schooling might include something from any or all disciplines, a selection of which disciplines to include at each stage is be made by teacher committees. In any case the integrity of each discipline is to be respected. Depending on the students' levels of learning at any point in time and their readiness for dealing with the more complex elements of a discipline, the arrangement of content within each discipline studied is to be made by the teacher of the given group of students. All this implies a carefully supervised continuum of content within each discipline from K to 12 governed by experts in each discipline. Only an illustrative sketch of how the curriculum might look in an actual school is presented in this book since work on its development must take place in each locality. Helpful chapters appear on the role of school leaders and others in accomplishing this work and on procedures for doing so.

The authors of this proposal give an extensive treatment of the history of the disciplines of knowledge (the autonomy and diversity of the disciplines) and their development and organization over time. They define a discipline as comprised of ten aspects: (1) as a community of discourse, (2) as an expression of human imagination, (3) as a domain of knowledge, (4) as an academic tradition, (5) as a syntactical structure or mode of inquiry, (6) as a conceptual structure or substantive realm of knowledge, (7) as a specialized language or system of symbols, (8) as a heritage of literature, artifacts, or network of communication, (9) as a valuative and affective stance, and (10) as an instructive community. With this understanding of a discipline, the curriculum of schooling in this proposal calls for students to be initiated into all aspects of this view of a discipline by the time they graduate.

Teaching Methods and Materials: Teachers of this proposed curriculum, in addition to meeting the ordinary criteria required of any competent teacher, must possess expertise in the specific discipline they are to teach. The ideal level of qualification necessary would seem to approach the level of the most competent disciplinary scholar in each field. However, the authors recognize several levels of limited expertise that teachers for K–12 schools could acquire and with which they could reasonably be matched to the level of pupil courses in the discipline they are assigned to teach. The implication is that teachers would continue to become schooled in their discipline to the highest level possible.

Teaching methods and materials used with K–12 students must conform to the processes and artifacts employed in the particular discipline. Teaching and using the inquiry methods appropriate to each discipline is, of course, central to this task. This does not imply ruling out proven methods of teaching content in general, but the emphasis is to be on employing the approaches used by those engaged in developing and advancing knowledge in the particular discipline. Bringing in visiting scholars as resident biologists or resident sociologists, for instance, is suggested. Allowing students to gain experience in utilizing the knowledge they have learned is certainly in keeping with this goal. The authors, however, do not seem to support non-disciplinary or interdisciplinary studies.

Program Evaluation: Very little is stated on this topic. The implied criterion for successful completion of the program is that a pupil can function like a little historian or a little linguist or a little chemist at some stated level.

Commentaries/Reviews/Critiques:

Arno A. Bellack, "The Structure of Knowledge and the Structure of the Curriculum," pp. 25–40 in Dwayne Huebner, ed., *A Reassessment of the Curriculum*. New York: Bureau of Publications, Teachers College, Columbia University, 1964.

Marion J. Kire, "The Case for the Disciplines. . .," ED 087 641, November 1972.

PROPOSAL 7

Phenix, Philip H., *Realms of Meaning: A Philosophy of the Curriculum for General Education.* New York: McGraw-Hill Book Company, 1964. 391 pp.

Focus: "The various patterns of knowledge are varieties of meaning, and the learning of these patterns is the clue to the effective realization of essential humanness through the curriculum of general education."

Unique Objective: "The full development of human beings requires education in a variety of realms of meaning rather than in a single type of rationality." The curriculum aims to "enlarge and deepen meaning," and to provide an integrated outlook, a coherent system of ideas, unity with an organic and comprehensive quality among diverse realms of meaning, and the power to experience essential patterns of meaning across all ways of knowing.

Program Organization: Six fundamental patterns of meaning emerge: symbolics, empirics, esthetics, synnoetics, ethics, and synoptics. Each of these has its subdisciplines and their typical methods of inquiry, leading ideas, and characteristic structures. Together they comprise the basic competencies that every person should develop "to satisfy the essential human need for meaning." Ordering and sequencing of these realms of meaning should be based on three factors: integrity of the disciplines to assure continuous progress at every stage of learning until wholeness of meaning is acquired, the logical order of the various kinds of meaning, and student level of development and maturity. There are probably many ways to organize the curriculum using this approach. The synoptic realm can lend itself to the use of an interdisciplinary organization better than other realms can while still maintaining the integrity of each discipline.

Symbolics is the realm of meaning that includes ordinary language, mathematics, and nondiscursive symbolic forms. Chapters are devoted to describing and summarizing the kinds of meaning developed in each of these disciplines.

(Note that this same type of information is presented for all the other realms of meaning included in the remainder of the book. The author does not attempt to identify all components of each discipline, but he orients the reader to this information in an analytic manner, gives the characteristic features and rationales for their different approaches to meaning, and points to references that more fully describe each discipline.)

Empirics is the realm of meaning that includes the physical sciences, biology, psychology, and the social sciences.

Esthetics is the realm of meaning that includes music, the visual arts, the arts of movement, and literature.

Synnoetics is the realm of meaning that includes personal knowledge or meanings "in which a person has direct insight into other beings (or oneself) as concrete wholes existing in relation." "Meanings in the synnoetic realm are subjective (and intersubjective), concrete, and existential."

Ethics is the realm of meaning that includes moral knowledge. It pertains to human rights, sex and family relations, and relations among social groups, issues of justice and power, and ideals and values.

Synoptics is the realm of meaning that includes history, religion, and philosophy.

The overall curriculum should embrace all these realms of meaning and their subdisciplines (others than those discussed are possible also). In addition to chapters on each or these realms of meaning, there are individual chapters devoted to the scope of the curriculum, to the logic of sequence in studies, and to developmental factors in the sequence of studies.

Selection of Content: The explosion of knowledge and the growing need for acquiring understanding and meaning create a huge problem for selection of content for the curriculum. To confront a sense of meaninglessness—"cynical doubt, fragmentation, surfeit, and pervasive transience," the author offers four principles of judicious selection of curriculum content applicable in all six realms of meaning.

First, select the most significant and consequential material only from the organized scholarly disciples.

Second, select the most representative or characteristic ideas from each discipline.

Third, select materials that exemplify the methods of inquiry in each discipline so that the student can actively engage with the subject.

Fourth, select content so that it will appeal to the imagination of the student at his or her level of maturity.

Teaching Methods and Materials: Little explicit guidance is given on this topic. However, a general rule is presented: "Many clues to effective mediation may be found within the disciplines themselves." "The teaching of material from any discipline should always be considered specifically in relation to the character of that discipline and not from some supposed principles of teaching in general."

Program Evaluation: This topic is not addressed in this proposal. Successful study of the realms of meaning is implied when the student progressively is able to reach the known knowledge in each of the disciplines.

Commentaries/Reviews/Critiques:

Chris Higgins and Seamus Mulryan, "Realms of Meaning," in Craig Kridel, ed., *Encyclopedia of Curriculum Studies*. Los Angeles, CA: Sage Publications, 2010. http://dx.doi.org/10.4135/9781412958806.n386

2

Partial Proposals with an Academic Focus

Bennett, William J., *James Madison High School: A Curriculum for American Students*. Washington, DC: United States Department of Education, 1987.
Bennett, William J., *James Madison Elementary School: A Curriculum for American Students*. Washington, DC: United States Department of Education, 1988.

To provide a common academic curriculum with rigorous standards for all students, not just the college bound.

* * *

Eisner, Elliot W., *Cognition and Curriculum: A Basis for Deciding What to Teach*. New York: Longman, 1982.
Eisner, Elliot W., *Cognition and Curriculum Reconsidered*. New York: Teachers College Press, 1994.

To focus the curriculum on the pursuit of meaning utilizing multiple forms of representation. Rather than relying exclusively on discursive and numerical forms of representation, the curriculum should also include expressive and mimetic forms of representation (poetic, literary, and metaphorical) and the fine arts (visual arts, music, dance, and drama).

* * *

Gardner, Howard, *Five Minds for the Future*. Boston, MA: Harvard Business Press, 2008.

To cultivate five capacities of the human mind: (1) The Disciplined Mind, (2) The Synthesizing Mind, (3) The Creative Mind, (4) The Respectful Mind, and (5) The Ethical Mind.

* * *

Hirsch, E. D., Jr., *Cultural Literacy: What Every American Needs to Know.* New York: Vintage Books, Random House, 1988. (Updated and Revised)

To acquire cultural literacy in the early years of schooling through a vocabulary-based and knowledge-based common core curriculum (rather than a skills-based curriculum)—later described as a Core Knowledge Sequence or communal knowledge.

Commentaries/Reviews/Critiques:
Core Knowledge Foundation, www.coreknowledge.org
Patrick Scott, *College English,* 50(March, 1988), 333–338.
Kristen L. Buras, *Harvard Educational Review,* 69(April, 1999), 67–93.
E. D. Hirsch, Jr., *The Schools We Need and Why We Don't Have Them.* New York: Anchor Books, Random House, 2010.
E. D. Hirsch, Jr., *Why Knowledge Matters: Rescuing Our Children from Failed Educational Theories.* Cambridge, MA: Harvard Education Press, 2016. Reviewed in *Educational Theory,* 67(No. 5, 2018), 639–647.
Emily Nemeth and Karen Graves, Chapter 17 in Joseph L. DeVitis, ed., *Popular Educational Classics: A Reader.* New York: Peter Lang, 2016.
Mike Schmoker, *Focus: Elevating the Essentials to Radically Improve Student Learning,* 2nd ed. Alexandria, VA: ASCD, 2018.

* * *

Koerner, James D., ed., *The Case for Basic Education: A Program of Aims for Public Schools.* Boston, MA: Little, Brown and Company, 1959.

To learn those subjects that have generative power (the major disciplines of knowledge) rather than those that are self-terminating (such as cooking, square-dancing, tying a tie). Generative subjects are used to learn other things throughout life. Several academics suggest what is basic in their fields of study: political science, history, geography, reading/writing/literature, languages, mathematics, and the sciences.

Review: *New York Review of Books,* February 1, 1963.

* * *

Parker, J. Cecil, and| Louis J. Rubin, *Process as Content: Curriculum Design and the Application of Knowledge.* Chicago, IL: Rand McNally & Company, 1966.

To teach the intellectual processes of the disciplines, not just their content (many of which have cross-disciplinary applications) and to teach how to use them in diverse contexts.

* * *

Reid, William A., "Democracy, Perfectibility, and the Battle of the Books: Liberal Education in the Writings of Schwab, " *Curriculum Inquiry*, 10(Autumn, 1980), 249–263.

To enable students to acquire a modern version of liberal education wherein the disciplines are used to aid students "to perfect themselves as social, political, moral, and intellectual agents." This author does not offer a curriculum proposal himself but highlights Joseph Schwab's version of liberal education, which he summarizes from Schwab's writings and places in the context of liberal education's historical roots in England and in the United States.

Part II

DEMOCRATIC-FOCUSED CURRICULUM PROPOSALS

3

Coherent Proposals with a Democratic Focus

PROPOSAL 8

Beane, James A., *Curriculum Integration: Designing the Core of Democratic Education*. New York: Teachers College Press, 1997. 122 pp.

Focus: The focus of this curriculum proposal is on integration of student experiences, on social integration, on integration of knowledge, and on integration as a curriculum design.

Unique Objective: To enhance "the possibilities of personal and social integration through the organization of curriculum around significant problems and issues, collaboratively identified by educators and young people, without regard for subject-area boundaries."

Program Organization: Curriculum integration is defined as a paradigm shift away from a subject-centered curriculum organization, away from teacher-centered methods of instruction, and away from a top-down measurement-oriented prescribed program toward an integration of several curriculum elements. It is guided by a philosophy of curriculum design that aims to integrate (1) the Self/Personal Concerns of students, (2) the Social/World issues seen by students, (3) four kinds of knowledge useful in addressing these concerns and issues (Personal, Social, Explanatory, and Technical Knowledge), and (4) concepts of Democracy, Dignity, and Diversity.

The basic structure of this curriculum is composed of Curriculum Themes chosen at the intersection of these four elements. Thus, an integrated curriculum visualized in this proposal cannot be set forth in advance of classroom decision-making by both students and teachers who make the choices of which Curriculum Themes to pursue and how to pursue them. It is a situationally designed curriculum—totally local in character. It can take a number of forms and follow a number of processes because it adheres to the choices made on the basis of the particular group of students and their personal needs to explore their own lives and the life of the world they recognize and participate in. The design for this integrated curriculum is diagramed and fully explained in chapter 4 of the proposal and is accompanied by examples of places where this type of curriculum has been employed.

Selection of Content: To choose the themes that will structure this kind of curriculum, students are asked to cooperatively select, with their teachers, the most significant themes to be pursued by the group. They are first asked to come up with answers to the question: *What questions or concerns do you have about yourself and your own life?* (Examples might be: Why do I fight with my brother and sister? Why do I have to go to school? Do other people think I am the way I think I am? What will I do to make a living when I finish school?) The students are also asked to come up with answers to the question: *What questions or concerns do you have about your world and public issues?* (Examples might be: How can we stop violence and murders in my town and elsewhere? Can we travel to and live on Mars? Where does garbage go? Can we stop global warming? On what does the government spend the most—or least—money?) These responses are examined to determine those shared by the group and of most significance for them to pursue. They will title these themes and be asked to decide how best to study them.

The model assumes that a process will be followed that includes investigating the questions inherent in the theme, locating the appropriate kind of knowledge that will illuminate the problem, using or applying that knowledge in coming to an understanding or resolution of the problem, and deciding what action should be taken to resolve the problem.

All this takes place within the framework of the philosophy of curriculum integration that honors and promotes the values of respect for individual dignity, democratic participation and practices, and critical thinking and analysis. The author of this proposal reports that the freedom of this approach engenders high interest, engagement, and learning by students.

Teaching Methods and Materials: The proposal provides examples of a number of approaches and activities appropriate for use in addressing chosen themes. However, there is not a great deal of direct guidance given about methods and materials. The assumption is that there are no "musts" and no "prohibitions" in this area. The role of the teacher is clearly to focus on facilitating the processes students will employ in following this model. Much knowledge of group processes, of sources of knowledge that can be drawn upon, of research procedures, and a mastery of critical thinking processes are among the skills that an integrated curriculum requires of a teacher in such a program. The author is conscious of the difficulties of implementing such an idealistic curriculum in the current atmosphere of public education, but he is convinced that the will to do so can be harnessed in many local settings using the professional knowledge readily available. His arguments are quite persuasive and he is quite confident and hopeful that more schools can adopt an integrated curriculum following this model.

Program Evaluation: This proposal does not address this topic.

Commentaries/Reviews/Critiques:

L. Thomas Hopkins and others, *Integration: Its Meaning and Application.* New York: Appleton-Century, 1937.

Marion Brady, *What's Worth Teaching?* Albany, NY: State University of New York Press, 1989.

James A. Beane, *A Middle School Curriculum: From Rhetoric to Reality.* 2nd ed. Columbus, OH: National Middle School Association, 1993.

James A. Beane, *Phi Delta Kappan* (April, 1995), 616–622.

Kenneth D. Jenkins and Doris M. Jenkins, *Middle School Journal,* 29(March, 1998), 14–27.

http://www.redorbit.com/news/education/199195/revisiting_curriculum_integration_a_fresh_look_at_an_old_idea/

Rethinking Schools - www.rethinkingschools.org

http://www.teachers.net/gazette/DEC00/varsbeane.html

Deborah Meier, Matthew Knoester, and Katherine Clunis D'Andrea, eds., *Teaching in Themes: An Approach to Schoolwide Learning, Creating Community, and Differentiating Instruction.* New York: Teaches College Press, 2015.

Brian D. Schultz, *Teaching in the Cracks: Openings and Opportunities for Student-Centered, Action-Focused Curriculum.* New York: Teachers College Press, 2017.

PROPOSAL 9

Hopkins, L. Thomas, *Interaction: The Democratic Process*. Boston, MA: D. C. Heath, 1941. 490 pp. Available online at: https://babel.hathitrust.org/cgi/pt?id=mdp.39015062752236;view=1up;seq=9

Focus: The teaching of democracy by means of experiencing the school as it operates as a democracy—based on beliefs and values of democratic living. (Chapter III identifies six of these.)

Unique Objective: To build better personalities and creative individuals who "grow to the maximum of their capacity," who learn to "develop cooperative interactive social action," who use conclusions drawn by others as "a datum not as a dictum," and who "believe in, respect, and utilize the appeal to reason in all social relationships."

Program Organization: This proposal does not designate any particular curriculum structure other than the use of curricular units and lessons. This is the result of its requirement that curriculum planning and design be done in situ through the participation of the particular pupils and adults involved. The author states that the scope and sequence of the program can be seen only after the curriculum has been completed; there is to be no preestablished scope and sequence.

Selection of Content: This proposed curriculum consists entirely of planned experiences that foster the goals of democratic education. Content is to be used instrumentally to achieve the learning of the various goals listed in the section above on its "Unique Objective." For the most part, these goals are social habits and skills that inhere within democratic beliefs and values (which are outlined and justified extensively throughout this book).

Some of these habits and skills around which educative experiences are to be planned and carried out are specified in this proposal. For example: (1) cooperating in the interactive processes of democratic decision-making, (2) acting on reasoned thinking, (3) selecting individual and social purposes on which to work, (4) managing educative experiences intelligently, (5) respecting the personality of others, and (6) evaluating learning in the process of experiencing. Others may be added to this list. Basic language skills are also to be included as needed.

The units and lessons that are chosen to be experienced, of course, need to be ordered in terms of personal and social significance and the current learning stages of the students. The book gives considerable guidance on these matters, including how experience units differ from subject matter units.

Teaching Methods and Materials: A lot of examples of teaching methods and materials appropriate to creating and utilizing student experiences to learn democratic habits and skills are included with this proposal. Also highlighted are necessary habits and skills that teachers should possess if they are to successfully guide these experiences in democracy. Schools that have complete or partial programs to teach democracy are cited throughout the book with examples of their features and experience units.

Program Evaluation: Chapter 10 is devoted to this topic. Democratic methods are stipulated.

Commentaries/Reviews/Critiques:

John Dewey, *Democracy and Education*. New York: The Macmillan Company, 1916.

Education Policies Commission, *The Unique Function of Education in American Democracy*. Washington, DC: National Education Association of the United States, 1937.

Harold Rugg, ed., *Democracy and the Curriculum*. New York: D. Appleton-Century Company, 1939.

Joseph Justman, *Bulletin of NASSP* (February 1942), 71–84.

James L. Mursell, *Principles of Democratic Education*. New York: W.W. Norton & Company, 1955.

Gertrude Noar, *Teaching and Learning the Democratic Way*. Englewood Cliffs, NJ: Prentice-Hall, 1963.

Ann Bastian, et al., *Choosing Equality: The Case for Democratic Schooling*. New York: The New World Foundation, 1985.

Michael W. Apple and James A. Beane, eds., *Democratic Schools*. Alexandria, VA: Association for Supervision and Curriculum Development, 1995.

Walter C. Parker, "Curriculum for Democracy," chapter 7 in Roger Soder, ed., *Democracy, Education, and the Schools*. San Francisco, CA: Jossey-Bass, 1996.

James A. Beane, *A Reason to Teach: The Power of the Democratic Way*. Portsmouth, NH: Heinemann, 2003.

John I. Goodlad, Roger Soder, and Bonnie McDaniel, eds., *Education and the Making of a Democratic People*. Boulder, CO: Paradigm Publishers, 2008.

Deborah Meier and Emily Gasoi, *The Schools Belong to You and Me: Why We Can't Afford to Abandon our Public Schools*. Boston, MA: Beacon Press, 2017.

PROPOSAL 10

White, John P., *Education and the Good Life: Autonomy, Altruism, and the National Curriculum*. New York: Teachers College Press, 1991. 190 pp.

Focus: A curriculum based on the ideals and values of a liberal democratic society.

Unique Objective: To ground the aims and content of curriculum in those personal qualities and understandings necessary "to prepare citizens for a life of autonomous well-being in a democratic society." These qualities and understandings are construed to embrace the virtues inherent in the overall educational aims of personal autonomy, altruistic well-being, and personal well-being.

Program Organization: This proposal does not offer a plan for organizing the curriculum. It advocates moving away from a knowledge-centered format to a values-centered format, and, consequently, a disciplines-oriented organization is not recommended. Local planners can utilize other structures so long as the three aims mentioned above are treated in an interrelated fashion and are not separately structured into a three-strand pattern. The emphasis on starting with democratic ideals and values, then moving to aims and content derived from these virtues, and then on to more detailed subdivisions and lessons does not imply, however, giving any less importance to the place of knowledge in the curriculum. The underlying ethical values are meant to justify the knowledge selected. Knowledge is to be used instrumentally to attain the value-aims. Knowledge-aims are not the starting point of this curriculum nor the basis for structuring the curriculum.

Selection of Content: The author of this proposal indicates that in order "to prepare citizens for a life of autonomous well-being in a democratic society" and to achieve the aims of "personal autonomy, altruistic well-being, and personal well-being," various capacities, dispositions, and types of understandings must be acquired by students. Deriving specific elements under each of these categories is left to local educators. However, lists of possible elements are discussed and justified in chapters devoted to each of the three broad aims and in outlining what the author means by "capacities, dispositions, and types of understandings."

For example, learning to obey classroom rules by young children is an appropriate capacity for that age level. It aids in developing a moral disposition necessary for living in a democratic society where citizens determine what rules they will live under and follow. Gradual acquiring of knowledge and understandings will later assist in making such judgments about particular public issues and policies, thus aiding in becoming an autonomous individual in a democratic society. Many other dispositions such as freedom, courage, respect for the dignity of human beings, protection of the rights of oneself and others, and openness to new ideas are discussed in detail. The author highlights the value of the arts and humanities in developing many of these dispositions.

Although the author makes this curriculum proposal in the context of urging a revision of the British National Curriculum, the aims and content, he rightly believes, are appropriate for any nation with a liberal democracy.

Teaching Methods and Materials: Throughout this proposal there are numerous comments on how teaching and learning would differ under this model from many of those presently in common use. Teachers might have to be reoriented from methods appropriate for teaching knowledge-based content to those appropriate for values-based content. Nevertheless, teaching and assessment approaches are left to local educators to determine based on the book's abundance of philosophically treated concepts related to democracy, values, dispositions, knowledge, autonomy, altruism, and the good life.

Program Evaluation: This topic is not treated in this proposal.

Commentaries/Reviews/Critiques:

Louis E. Raths, et al., *Values and Teaching*. Columbus, OH: Merrill, 1st ed. 1966; 2nd ed. 1978.

John White, *Impact No. 1*, 2007. http://onlinelibrary.wiley.com/doi/10.1111/j.2048-416X.2007.tb00116.x/epdf

D. C. Mulcahy, *The Educated Person: Toward a New Paradigm for Liberal Education*. Lanham, MD: Rowman & Littlefield Publishers, 2008.

John White, *Education Review*, 19(No. 1, 2008).

Alan L. Lockwood, *The Case for Character Education*. New York: Teachers College Press, 2009.

Michael J. Reiss and John White, *An Aims-based Curriculum: The Significance of Human Flourishing for the Schools*. London, UK: Institute of Education Press, University of London, 2013.

4

Partial Proposals with a Democratic Focus

Banks, James A., *An Introduction to Multicultural Education*, 6th ed. Especially Chapters 3. 4, and 5. New York: Pearson, 2019.

To help students acquire the knowledge, skills, and attitudes needed to function as effective citizens in a diverse nation and world.

* * *

Brameld, Theodore, *Design for America: An Educational Exploration of the Future of Democracy*. New York; Hinds, Hayden & Eldredge, 1945.

To engage as students in the cooperative planning of the future of our democratic society in terms of its economic, political, artistic, science, education, and human relations institutions. Includes a report of Floodwood (Minnesota) High School that undertook such a project.

* * *

Educational Policies Commission, *The Purposes of Education in American Democracy*. Washington, DC: National Education Association of the United States, 1938.

To educate in four areas of common objectives: (1) Self-Realization, (2) Human Relationships, (3) Economic Efficiency, and (4) Civic Responsibility.

* * *

Goodlad, John I., and Thomas C. Lovitt, eds., *Integrating General and Special Education.* New York: Macmillan, 1993 (especially Chapters 4 and 6).

To integrate students with special needs into a comprehensive system of education that includes all students having rights to a normal public education. The proposal is based on eight postulates and their corollaries that form a framework for this kind of balanced and equitable curriculum.

* * *

Grant, Carl A., "Cultivating Flourishing Lives: A Robust Social Justice Vision of Education*," American Educational Research Journal,* 49(Issue 5, 2012), 910–934.

To learn to engage in action for social justice in a multicultural environment. This includes five core practices: (1) self-assessment, (2) critical questioning, (3) the practice of democracy, (4) social action, and (5) tools of adjudication.

* * *

McLaren, Peter, "Critical Pedagogy: A Look at the Major Concepts," pp. 194–223 in Peter McLaren, *Life in Schools: An Introduction to Critical Pedagogy in the Foundations of Education,* 5th ed. Boston, MA: Pearson Education, 2007.

To learn to question the dominant themes in the taken-for-granted knowledge residing in the curriculum and in the hidden curriculum of the school; to learn to take political action for causes deemed worthy. Though not cast in curricular terms, this proposal implies how the curriculum can be constructed and presented.

Commentaries/Reviews/Critiques:
E. Wayne Ross, Chapter 19 in Joseph L. DeVitis, ed., *Popular Educational Classics: A Reader.* New York: Peter Lang, 2016.

* * *

Miller, Ron, Free Schools, *Free People: Education and Democracy after the 1960s.* Albany, NY: State University of New York Press, 2002.

To foster existential authenticity rather than technocracy via a free school ideology. This proposal describes the free school movement of the 1960s and highlights its salient features for the future of democratic education.

* * *

Newmann, Fred M., *Education for Citizen Action: Challenge for Secondary Curriculum*. Berkeley, CA: McCutchan Publishing Corporation, 1975.

To enhance a high school student's ability to exert influence in public affairs and public policy through academic studies and social action projects. Components of this proposal include the study of moral deliberation, social policy research, political-legal processes, advocacy, group process, organizational management, and psycho-philosophical concerns.

Commentaries/Reviews/Critiques:
Meira Levinson, *No Citizen Left Behind*. Cambridge, MA: Harvard University Press, 2012.
Joel Westheimer, *What Kind of Citizen? Educating Our Children for the Common Good*. New York: Teachers College Press, 2015.

* * *

Rebell, Michael A., *Flunking Democracy: Schools, Courts, and Civic Participation*. Chapter 4. Chicago, IL: University of Chicago Press, 2018.

To provide a curriculum for learning to participate in a deliberative democracy that emphasizes civic knowledge, verbal and cognitive skills, critical analytic skills, and fundamental values of character.

Part III

GLOBAL-FOCUSED CURRICULUM PROPOSALS

5

Coherent Proposals with a Global Focus

PROPOSAL 11

Goodlad, John I., and Associates, *Toward a Mankind School: An Adventure in Humanistic Education*. New York: McGraw-Hill, 1974. 193 pp.

Focus: On the process of operating a global system of interacting people and societies—*A Mankind Curriculum*—where understanding mankind is a unifying concept for the whole curriculum. "Mankind" in this proposal encompasses "all people and their institutions, all nations and religions, all cultures and civilizations, past and present, and in anticipation of their future."

Unique Objective: To attain awareness and understanding of mankind and its functioning and to learn to commit to acting upon it rationally, critically, and effectively.

Program Organization: Student experiences would include: (1) The Study of Mankind, (2) The Study of Human Interactions, (3) The Culture of the School, and (4) Traditional Subject Matters with a Mankind Focus.

Seven broad phases of education would constitute the general structure of the program: Early Childhood, Lower Elementary, Upper Elementary, Middle School, High School, Post-High School, and Continuing Life. Each of these phases would include experiences appropriate to that age group and drawn from all four of the above components.

Selection of Content: The proposal suggests possible experiences for each phase and component of this program structure. It also gives examples from schools that have such programs. Local educators and the students would, however, choose the array of content and determine its placement at the various phases. The major rule governing this process is to assure that the content contributes to acquiring a Mankind Perspective. Certain values, assumptions, and criteria for selecting subject matter are provided in chapter 4.

Teaching Methods and Materials: This type of curriculum would be person-oriented, and students would make decisions about their learning and be allowed to progress at their individual pace. Group- or grade-oriented teaching would not be common, and, therefore, teaching methods would be adapted to the primary learning method of student interactions and experiences. Much interdisciplinary work would be expected. Again, the proposal gives examples of activities and plans from schools.

Program Evaluation: No special treatment is given to this topic.

Commentaries/Reviews/Critiques:

Ulich, Robert, ed., *Education and the Idea of Mankind*. New York: Harper Brothers, 1964.

Gaudelli, William, *World Class Teaching and Learning in Global Times*. Mahwah, NJ: Lawrence Erlbaum Associates, 2003.

Subedi, Binaya, "Decolonizing the Curriculum for Global Perspectives," *Educational Theory,* 63(December, 2013), 621–648.

Gaudelli, William, *Global Citizenship Education: Everyday Transcendence*. New York: Routledge, 2016.

PROPOSAL 12

O'Sullivan, Edmund, *Transformative Learning: Educational Vision for the 21st Century*. New York: Zed Books and Toronto: University of Toronto Press, 1999. 304 pp.

Focus: Educating for full planetary consciousness

Unique Objective: To foster a new world-view (a new cosmology) that recognizes the interrelationships among human beings and all features of our universe (living and nonliving) —the "web of life"—and "an ecologically sustainable vision of society." "Our world is sending us distress signals" as a result of humanity's false world-view of globalization and pillage of the world's resources. We need to learn how to relate harmoniously with the natural elements and with all living things on the planet. Our survival and the survival of society depends on our recovering the sense of wholeness that our present cosmology does not let us see and then acting in accord with that new world-view. Instances of violence to the planet and of ills to society resulting from our actions are reviewed. Examples of efforts to educate for this new "ecozoic" vision are also presented.

Program Organization: No particular plan is presented in this proposal. "I feel that the specificity of contexts demands the specific creativity of the people or communities who live and work and educate in those contexts." What is presented is essentially an educational vision with guiding principles and suggested content that local teachers and curriculum planners can use to design their own curriculum.

Selection of Content: Courses for higher education that are suggested include: (1) the sequence of evolutionary process phases that the story of the universe embraces, (2) human development and its variations including the development of personal identities over the ages, (3) cultures that have dominated human development in the past and present, (4) the rise of the scientific/ rationalistic/technological world-view and its consequences, (5) the emerging ecozoic period, the biosphere, and the healing of the planet, and (6) the origin and identification of human values within our experience of the universe.

Study of the unfolding processes of the universe is also essential at the high school level, backed up by studies in astronomy, earth science, life sciences, earth history, ecological literacy, the bio-region in which students live. Childhood education should provide stories of awe, wonder, beauty, and interrelatedness of the universe.

While no comprehensive structure for implementing this vision of ecological education is laid out in this proposal, there are a myriad of content resources described here for use in selecting content and designing programs.

In addition, carefully argued rationales for the vision presented are to be found throughout the book. Guiding concepts also appear, such as community, diversity, dreams of the future, transformative rather than reformative, combining of the intellectual/the emotional/the moral/and the spiritual, ecozoic rather than cenozoic, wholeness, peace/nonviolence, etc.

Teaching Methods and Materials: Very little is discussed.
Program Evaluation: No guidance is provided.
Commentaries/Reviews/Critiques:

Thomas Berry, *The Dream of the Earth*. San Francisco: Sierra Club Books, 1988.

Brian Swimme and Thomas Berry, *The Universe Story: An Autobiography from Planet Earth*. San Francisco: Harper and Row, 1992.

Mary Ann O'Connor, *Convergence,* 33(2000), 158–161,

Lynn Speer Lemisko, *Canadian Social Studies*, 37(Winter, 2003).

http://legacy.oise.utoronto.ca/research/tlcentre/books/transformative.html?cms_page=books/transformative.html

6

Partial Proposals with a Global Focus

Braus, Judy A., and David Wood, *Environmental Education in the Schools: Creating a Program that Works*. Troy, OH: North American Association for Environmental Education, 1994. Also online at: https://babel.hathitrust.org/cgi/pt?id=mdp.39015034873318;view=1up;seq=512

To infuse a comprehensive environmental education program into the curriculum. Has models, rationales, procedures, and many illustrative courses, lessons, and activities.

Commentaries/Reviews/Critiques:
Donald E. Hawkins and Dennis A. Vinton, *The Environmental Classroom*. Englewood Cliffs, NJ: Prentice-Hall, Inc., 1973.
C. A. Bowers, *Educating for an Ecologically Sustainable Culture*. Chapter 7. Albany, NY: State University of New York Press, 1985.
World Commission on Environment and Development, *Our Common Future*. Oxford, UK: Oxford University Press, 1987.
Joy Palmer and Philip Neal, eds., *The Handbook of Environmental Education*. New York: Routledge, 1995.
C. A. Bowers, *Educating for Eco-Justice and Community*. Chapter 4. Athens, GA: University of Georgia Press, 2001.

***

Robinson, Ken, *Creative Schools: The Grassroots Revolution That's Transforming Education*. New York: Viking, 2015. Related but slightly different: Michael Fullan, Joanne Quinn, and Joanne McEachen, *Deep Learning: Engage the World, Change the World*. Thousand Oaks, CA: Corwin, 2018.

To provide a customized approach to curriculum based on four educational purposes (economic, cultural, social, personal) requiring the development of eight kinds of abilities (curiosity, creativity, criticism, communication, collaboration compassion, composure, and citizenship).

Commentaries/Reviews/Critiques:
www.ndpl.global
Ontario Ministry of Education, "Achieving Excellence: A Renewed Vision for Education Ontario, 2014." www.edu.gov.on.ca.eng/about/renewedvision.pdf

* * *

Santone, Susan, *Reframing the Curriculum: Design for Social Justice and Sustainability*. New York: Routledge & Kappa Delta Pi, 2019

To educate for social justice and sustainability through addressing transdisciplinary topics, social consciousness, equity/ethics, diversity, and well-being. Gives multiple suggested content and teaching approaches.

* * *

Waks, Leonard J., *Education 2.0: The Learningweb Revolution and the Transformation of the School*. Boulder, CO: Paradigm Publishers, 2014.

To offer high school and older students limitless subject matters in a variety of forms, including via the internet and other media. This proposal utilizes Open Learning Centers organized for self-directed independent study and enriched learning experiences and calls for facilitation by professionals in teaching and content media through a whole new open structure for education.

Part IV

LIVING-FOCUSED CURRICULUM PROPOSALS

7

Coherent Proposals with a Living Focus

PROPOSAL 13

James, Charity, *Young Lives at Stake: The Education of Adolescents*. New York: Agathon Press, 1972. 258 pp.

Focus: A person-centered, collaborative, open and living curriculum as a basis for an "Education for a Well-spent Youth."

Unique Objective: To actively engage in interdisciplinary inquiry, making, and dialogue by exploring, experimenting, or explaining significant nondisciplinary questions chosen by students themselves in collaboration with their teachers.

The author gives considerable attention to defining, explaining, and justifying these three dimensions of a curriculum for youth (ages 11–18) in the context of education in England but clearly stating its appropriateness for schools in the United States and elsewhere. It is included here as a possible model for K–12 curriculum because it has direct implications for early and elementary education (though it does not discuss these levels of education) and would depend on such a foundation consistent with the focus it prescribes for the adolescent years. This earlier curriculum would need to be developed by those adopting this model.

Fundamental to this proposal is attention to conducting "interdisciplinary inquiry and making" as the way that most closely matches the learning modes of youth and most directly provides the processes and concepts needed to face life problems and situations, currently and in the future. Disciplinary studies are given subordinate status to interdisciplinary studies in this curriculum. "Dialogue" by students and others is the means of doing all this inquiry in a collaborative fashion rather than employing direct instruction by teachers or others.

The portion of the curriculum devoted to "interdisciplinary inquiry" is based on the notion that most questions that arise in life must be addressed with more than one discipline, and thus practice in this form of inquiry is more functional than learning to do (or to understand the results of) disciplinary inquiry.

"Interdisciplinary making" is defined as that productive and critical thinking (rather than mere doing or redoing what others have made or done) that engages the student's creativity in making or creating something new. It is realistic and calls forth intentional and purposeful action. It is coupled in this curriculum proposal with interdisciplinary inquiry so that it does not focus solely on one discipline or another as a constraint to creative making or doing. This type of learning is not limited to the arts or technologies but can and should draw on any or all disciplines. As noted in the next section, disciplinary inquiry is not ignored in this proposal; it is studied as a source for interdisciplinary inquiry and making.

Program Organization: A fourfold curriculum organization is incorporated into this proposal: (1) Interdisciplinary Studies, (2) Autonomous Studies, (3) Remedial Education, and (4) Special Interest Studies.

The first of these includes both interdisciplinary inquiry and interdisciplinary making. This component comprises about 50 percent of the day at the level of age 11 and by age 18 perhaps only about 20 percent. Autonomous Studies are those devoted to one or more of the disciplines and increases from a relatively small portion of the day at age 11 to a relatively large portion by age 18. However, in the upper range of years much of the disciplinary studies could be included in Special Interest Studies depending upon the individual student's occupational or pre-professional goals. Only those features of disciplinary studies that support the interdisciplinary inquiry and making would be included in Autonomous Studies. Most of this component would be conducted by the same group of students engaged in an interdisciplinary investigation, focusing collaboratively on their need for this disciplinary knowledge. Remedial Education would occur in a clinic where the individual catch-up learning would be provided by "peripatetic teachers." The Special Interest Studies section of the curriculum is time during which students can follow their personal interests in almost any activity or study with faculty support and guidance.

All four of these components are to be included in every year of a student's program in varying amounts of time as the years progress.

Selection of Content: "Areas of investigation" would be chosen largely by local educators working collaboratively at each level to devise options from which groups of students and teachers would collaboratively choose "specific inquiry questions to work on" at given times during the school year. Such a predetermined array of areas of investigation would serve merely as a resource and not as a prescribed list. Students and teachers could come up with new topics and questions at any time or could choose from this list. The point is to have as flexible and open a curriculum as possible where immediate choice is given highest priority. As examples of areas of investigation, the author mentions for age 11 "Man the Explorer" and "Growing Up." Inquiry questions within these could be quite numerous but would be chosen by the students and their teachers as would choices of creative interdisciplinary making projects within such areas. There is no intention in this proposal that any preplanned curriculum problems or content would be followed. Student needs and interests would determine what is studied at any given time. Extensive resources that could be drawn upon by students as they do their inquiry and related work would be necessary to permit this model to succeed. The author provides quite a bit of help related to options and choices for each age level. There is also help provided for components two, three, and four of the proposed curriculum.

Teaching Methods and Materials: In addition to the task mentioned above of collecting and organizing an array of possible areas and questions for investigation, teachers would organize clusters of students to work on a given task and provide assistance as they proceed with their work. There would be no "classes" with a teacher assigned permanently to a "class." "Clusters" of students with an associated teacher or teachers would be set up as needed and discharged when their work is completed. That could happen after four or five days, or after a month, or after a longer period depending upon the nature of the work. New clusters and topics to work on would be devised periodically. The author suggests having a main group of perhaps 150 students, with divisions of about thirty-five, and clusters of five to seven students. Each category would have assigned teachers and other educators to provide organizational assistance, collaborative decision-making, pedagogical assistance, and student appraisals.

This kind of plan calls for a very different role for teachers than is common in most schools today. With little or no teacher-directed instruction in this model, teachers assume the role of enablers. They must be experienced in processes of inquiry and creativity. They must be able to guide students in those processes. They must be open and flexible in collaborating with students in decision-making and supporting them in their work. There would have to be some teachers who are specialists in one or more disciplines, but most teachers would have to be experts in dealing with interdisciplinary questions as well as competent in understanding the needs and interests of particular age-level students. The traditional concept of teaching methods and materials is somewhat inappropriate in this kind of curriculum. Nonetheless, the skills and knowledge necessary to be a competent enabler are many and need to be readily at hand.

Program Evaluation: A short section of this book deals with program evaluation.

Commentaries/Reviews/Critiques:

Karne Kozolanka, "An Appreciation of 'Making' Activities." ERIC Document ED 368 688, 1994.

Alfred North Whitehead, *The Aims of Education*. New York: Mentor Books, 1929.

James B. Macdonald, *Journal of Curriculum Theorizing,* 3(No. 1, 1981), 143–153. Reprinted in Bradley J. Macdonald, ed., *Theory as a Prayerful Act: The Collected Essays of James B. Macdonald*. New York: Peter Lang, 1995.

PROPOSAL 14

Prensky, Marc, *Education to Better Their World: Unleashing the Power of 21st-Century Kids*. New York: Teachers College Press, 2016. 134 pp.

Focus: An "accomplishment-based" approach rather than an academic-based approach.

Unique Objective: "To empower all kids to be able to take action to improve their own world and to see themselves as having agency." This proposal is named, A Better-Their-World Education, and emphasizes the production by every student (often in teams) of real-world accomplishments that improve the world, not just individual student achievements in academic studies. A large portion of this proposal is devoted to distinguishing between an individually achieved, academically based curriculum (such as is now common) and one that is personally oriented but "accomplishment-based," the latter of which is the focus of this explicitly spelled-out and thoroughly argued proposal.

This proposal calls for students to identify and to work on real-world projects in order to accomplish project goals and thereby improve the world in some significant ways. By completing dozens of such projects during their K–12 education, they become empowered to deal successfully with their world immediately and not just after completion of their entire span of K–12 education.

Program Organization: In this vision of a new kind of education, the proposed curriculum must, therefore, focus on accruing "real-world accomplishments." Priority is given to having students personally and freely choose to carry out projects that result in changes in the real world. They focus on what they are passionate to accomplish in their world. Their accomplishing of these particular kinds of goals are recorded in their resumes (not grades in subjects), which also indicate the skills acquired that were needed to accomplish the project goals.

The author of this proposal gives a partial list of types of projects that might be undertaken by students: (1) Projects to help your local community (creating local parks or gardens), (2) Projects to help the less fortunate (redistributing discarded materials), (3) Projects to help build and repair infrastructure (putting in Wi-Fi and Internet connections), (4) Projects to directly assist peers or others (working with senior citizens), (5) Projects to help preserve our history and legacy (digitizing texts), (6) Projects to assist with government functions (measuring air and water quality), (7) Projects adding new information to the world's knowledge and databases (inventions and innovations), and Projects for public service (evaluating public services and personnel).

This project organization does not stand alone as the total structure of the proposed curriculum. To it must be added key skills in four areas: (1) Effective Thinking Skills, (2) Effective Action Skills, (3) Effective Relationship Skills, and (4) Effective Accomplishment Skills. Each of these types of skills is defined, listed, and illustrated in the proposal. How they may be applied to conducting various projects is also illustrated. They are not "taught" in special courses or lessons; they are integrated into the work of accomplishing the particular projects that a student is undertaking. References to schools currently doing this kind of curriculum are listed throughout the proposal.

Note that the organization of the school day for both students and teachers will be very open and flexible in this type of program. Much work will be done in time and space convenient for individual students (often perhaps not at school). Groups of students working together on a project will need special time and space arrangements, and their teachers will need to be scheduled accordingly.

Selection of Content: Selection of content is made by the student as needed for the project at hand. The use of technology to convey needed information, visual artifacts, or other relevant teaching of skills is to be available to the student in banks of preestablished resources through the Internet and created by either their teachers or consortiums of educators.

Teaching Methods and Materials: The role of the teacher in this kind of curriculum is to be a coach or guide who empowers students to successfully accomplish their real-world project goals. A full chapter is devoted to discussing the role of teachers (who in this model are not content deliverers). A special kind of teacher education will be necessary to prepare teachers for a curriculum intended to improve the world rather than to foster academic skills and knowledge.

A major function of teachers and other educators in this model is to see that appropriate resource banks of project ideas, skills instruction, and relevant content are available in all areas mentioned above for the curriculum (thinking, action, relationships, and accomplishing). Organizing all this for appropriate maturity levels from primary to secondary schooling will also be required. Doing all this is no small task. Accumulated sharing of these resources will eventually lessen the burden as more and more schools adopt this "accomplishments model." Nevertheless, there will also be times when teachers must give direct instruction as well as coach and supervise students in their projects.

Program Evaluation: Very little is said on this topic in this proposal. It is evident, however, that student accomplishments will need to be well documented for the quality of their work and that this will be useful in gaging any particular student's level of competence at any point in his school years as well as at the end. It will be difficult to claim that this curriculum failed no matter the level of students' accomplishments.

Commentaries/Reviews/Critiques:
www.global-future-education.org

PROPOSAL 15

Stratemeyer, Florence B., Hamden L. Forkner, Margaret G. McKim, and A. Harry Passow, *Developing a Curriculum for Modern Living*, 1st ed. New York: Bureau of Publications, Teachers College, Columbia University, 1947. 2nd ed, revised and enlarged, 1957. 740 pp.

Stratemeyer, Florence B., with Margaret G. McKim and Mayme Sweet, *Guides to a Curriculum for Modern Living*. New York: Bureau of Publications, Teachers College, Columbia University, n.d. 60 pp.

Focus: Learning to cope with Persistent Life Situations through the daily life concerns of children and youth

Unique Objective: Proposes "a curriculum that develops maximum effectiveness in meeting the problems of modern living by making use of the immediate situations learners face as a basis for developing competencies and understandings for future action." Persistent Life Situations are "those situations that recur in the life of individuals in many different ways as they grow from infancy to maturity." For example, keeping well, making a living, getting along with others, dealing with social and political structures and forces, or grasping the ever-changing world of knowledge and thought. Pupils participate in such Persistent Life Situations at the level of their present development and through mastery of these current situations become able to master ever more complex situations as their life proceeds. The skills and understandings thus acquired by successful accomplishment at each stage of development of a particular Persistent Life Situation serve to equip them to cope with later stages and with novel situations that will be faced throughout life.

Program Organization: Proposed are four main categories of Persistent Life Situations around which this curriculum is to be organized:

(1) Individual and Group Situations of Everyday Living (Family, Civic, Social Activities, Work, Leisure, Spiritual Life)
(2) Situations Involving Growth in Individual Capacities (Health, Intellectual Power, Moral Choices, Aesthetic Expression and Appreciation)
(3) Situations Involving Growth in Social Participation (Person-to-Person Relations, Group Membership, Intergroup Relations)
(4) Situations Involving Growth in Ability to Deal with Environmental Factors and Forces (Natural Phenomena, Technological Resources, Economic-Social-Political Structures and Forces).

One hundred fifty pages of this proposal are devoted to defining and illustrating typical situations of daily living in each of these categories and subcategories. These examples are divided into four groupings that identify situations typical of concerns at the Early Childhood Stage, the Later Childhood Stage, the Youth Stage, and the Adulthood Stage.

A rationale is given by the authors for each and every typical situation presented and for the broader treatment of the scope and sequence of this entire curriculum with its basis in democratic values, human development research, and teaching and learning theory. It would be difficult to locate another curriculum proposal that provides such a thorough and clearly argued rationale for its overall vision and its many diverse elements. That said, it is less prescriptive than it may at first appear to be. The authors intend this to be a framework for a curriculum using Persistent Life Situations as its focus, but they urge that any of their detailed subsituations within these four broad categories might be tailored to the priorities seen in a local situation or might be changed or added to as time passes and new Persistent Life Situations emerge.

To catch a glimpse of the detailed resources that are presented in this proposal (before reading the entire 740 pages of this book), it may be helpful to excerpt examples from one section of the proposal as an illustration of what can be found throughout the proposal.

Under category 2 above, Individual Capacities, the section on Intellectual Power, for instance, includes the following:

---

(1) Making Ideas Clear

Using Language to Communicate Ideas	Contributing to informal discussions and conversations
	Making oral presentations
	Expressing ideas in written form
Using Media other than Language to Express Ideas	Using graphic forms
	Using aesthetic forms

(2) Understanding the Ideas of Others

Reading	Using appropriate reading approach
	Using source materials
	Interpreting graphic presentations
Listening	Following and evaluating informal discussions and conversations
	Following and evaluating oral presentations
	Understanding musical and dramatic forms of expression
Observing	Interpreting environmental surroundings

(Continued)

(3) Dealing with Quantitative Relationships

Interpreting Number Values and Symbols	Understanding symbols and relationships
Computing	Estimating amounts
	Making exact computations
	Using measuring instruments

(4) Using Effective Methods of Work

Planning	Deciding on and clarifying purpose
	Determining sequence of steps to achieve purpose
	Budgeting time and energy
	Evaluating steps taken
Using Appropriate Resources	Locating and evaluating the resource
Using a Scientific Approach to the Study of Situations	Solving practical problems
	Testing beliefs and attitudes

Note that for each of the typical situations in the right-hand column above further breakdowns for the four Stages of Life can be found. For example, under (1) Using media other than language to express ideas, for using graphic forms, the illustrative situation given for Early Childhood Stage is: Using pictorial forms of expression; for Later Childhood Stage: Understanding the uses of common forms of graphic expression; for Youth Stage: Extending the range of uses and variety of forms of graphic expression; for Adulthood Stage: Using forms of graphic expression appropriate to a variety of purposes. Under each of these can be found several examples of suitable activities that will engage pupils in learning to cope with the typical situation.

Selection of Content: This task is left to the teacher to determine with respect to the stage of life of the pupils and through discernment of the current daily living concerns of the pupils in their classroom.

The overall choice of which Persistent Life Situations to deal with at which specific points in the curriculum is also to be left to the teacher to determine. The book has whole chapters of guidance to offer in this regard in keeping with the values and assumptions stated in the rationale for this proposal.

The comprehensive framework of situations presented in this book (which includes 164 different Persistent Life Situations in twenty-nine categories—remember these are illustrative, not prescriptive) does not necessarily imply that all of these must be dealt with in every class of pupils at all four stages of development; what is to be dealt with will depend on the concerns of the students at their point in life. Nevertheless, this framework can serve as a check on whether some situations have been neglected or overlooked in the full range of experiences that are provided for pupils.

Teaching Methods and Materials: Several chapters of this book are devoted to discussing how to select and guide the experiences of pupils in keeping with the principles underlying this proposal. Clearly this proposal is dedicated to meeting individual differences among pupils as well as to affording them the opportunities needed to learn to cope with typical situations of living as individuals and as members of society.

Most helpful are chapters 12, 13, and 14 which give detailed guidance on what teachers can do in a year's time with a first-grade class, with a fifth-grade class, and with a tenth-grade class. The supplementary booklet cited with this book title above also addresses these same issues for the benefit of teachers and includes helps for other grade levels as well.

Teachers who are able to teach this kind of curriculum have to be generalists and quite versatile. Teacher-pupil planning is essential. Cooperative teaching can sometimes be utilized when teachers are not broadly capable of dealing with all kinds of life situations, but this requires that all teachers involved know their pupils well.

Program Evaluation: An entire chapter is devoted to "making evaluation an integral part of the curriculum." The test of whether a program based on this proposal has been successful in preparing pupils to cope with Persistent Life Situations is to be based on careful research done to answer a set of questions listed on pages 512–513. Data on related topics such as administrative support, school-community relations, and the actions of children, youth, and adults in coping with Persistent Life Situations are also required if a complete program evaluation is to be done.

Commentaries/Reviews/Critiques:
Ole Sand, *The Elementary School Journal*, 48(February, 1948), 344–346.
William B. Featherstone, *A Functional Curriculum for Youth*. New York: American Book Company, 1950.
Richard W. Burkhart, *The Educational Forum*, 17(May, 1953), 486–487.

PROPOSAL 16

Totten, W. Fred, and Frank J. Manley, *The Community School: Basic Concepts, Function, and Organization*. Galien, MI: Allied Education Council, 1969. 278 pp.

Focus: A community-centered program for all members of the community (all ages, not just school-age children) that operates 24/7/365 and focuses not only on academic and practical studies but on services needed by students and community members such as food, clothing, shelter, employment, and other social and civic services—all under the administration of the school.

Unique Objective: To use the broad resources of the community in the education of individuals throughout their lives and in the improvement of society through cooperative resolution of community problems and taking cooperative action to fulfill the wishes of the community as a whole.

This proposal is the one that helps unify the home, school, and community. It helps overcome barriers to social progress by getting community members, young and old, involved and informed. It serves people from cradle to grave including the period of formal education (Pre-K to 12) where the curriculum may be similar to that operating in many other schools but which has the added function of focusing on discovering the students' own problems and needs as well as those of the larger community, on explaining or formulating possible solutions to these concerns, and on applying the results in practical, real-life situations. It stimulates healthy living. It provides leisure-time activities for both children and adults. It provides culturally enriching experiences for all who wish to participate. It raises literacy levels in adults who missed learning this earlier in life. It becomes a setting for the practice of freedom and democratic citizenship. The school becomes the center of activity—educationally, socially, recreationally, and culturally. It leads in individual and community development.

Examples of community schools in operation are cited throughout this proposal—primarily from Flint, Michigan, with which the authors were affiliated, but also from several other school systems.

Program Organization: No one way to organize the program of a community school is visualized in this proposal. It is expected that each local school system will devise its own workable approach. Ordinarily, the structure is conceived as a set of multiple programs, each devoted to a set of people with special concerns and addressed to a short-term topic or need. Therefore, it involves a process of continuous planning for changing groups and varying purposes.

The proposal says little about how to organize the "required program" for the ordinary schooling of children and youth. (Presumably one would rely on student or community advice about such decisions.) The proposal, however, gives several illustrations of how to structure "optional programs" for people of all ages where the assumption is that these programs will come and go and new optional programs will constantly be provided as the need for them is discerned.

Selection of Content: The appendix to this proposal gives suggested areas of content for the "optional program" whose purposes are listed as follows: "1) improve mental and physical health, 2) upgrade the educational level of the people, 3) improve citizenship, 4) improve academic performance of children and youth, 5) bring about a united front for democratic action, 6) improve living conditions in general, 7) break down barriers to social progress, 8) upgrade people economically, and 9) in general, diminish the harm done by delinquency, school dropouts, poverty, racial segregation, and unemployment."

From the appendix, here are selected examples of content areas suggested:

For the Unborn and Infants:	Parent classes in prenatal care
Programs for Children:	Recreational and Social—free play in gym, square dancing, parties
	Cultural and Aesthetic—choral groups, crafts, creative drama
	Academic—science fairs, typing, tutoring assistance
	General—story hour, breakfast
	Summer Programs—baseball leagues, camp, farm visits
	Health Programs—activities for handicapped, dental inspection, update health records
Programs for Youth:	Recreational, Athletics, and Social—bike hikes, sports in season, dinners
	Cultural—concerts, tours, trips
	Academic—debate, intensive study, work experience
	General—tutoring younger children, teen traffic court, music camp
	Community Service Programs—volunteer traffic directing, clean –up campaigns, serve on civic committees
Programs for Adults:	Academic—credit courses, home arts, retailing, construction, horticulture
	Recreational and Social—dancing, swimming, potlucks, bridge, social clubs
	Cultural and Aesthetic—book clubs, concerts, tours, trips, town hall meetings
	General—skills retraining, emotional recovery meetings
	Senior Citizens—arm-chair travelogues, potluck suppers, service projects
	Family Life, Service, Citizenship—child study classes, big brother programs, leadership training

Teaching Methods and Materials: Little discussion of these topics is provided.

Program Evaluation: No specific guidance is given.

Commentaries/Reviews/Critiques:

http://www.communityschools.org

Elsie Ripley Clapp, *Community Schools in Action*. New York: Viking Press, 1939.

Nelson B. Henry, ed., *The Community School*. 52nd Yearbook of the National Society for the Study of Education, Part II. Chicago: The University of Chicago Press, 1953.

Edward G. Olsen, ed., *School and Community*, 2nd ed. New York: Prentice–Hall, 1954.

Barbara Hunt, Introduction to the Community School Concept. ERIC Doc 030 185 1968.

http://www.nea.org/assets/docs/Comm%20Schools%20ToolKit-final%20digi-web-5-23-17.pdf

Joy G. Dryfoos and Sue Maguire, *Inside Full-Service Community Schools*. Thousand Oaks, CA: Corwin Press, 2002.

Lee Benson, et al., "The Enduring Appeal of Community Schools," *American Educator*, 33(Summer, 2009), 22–47.

Strike, Kenneth A., *Small Schools and Strong Communities: A Third Way of School Reform*. New York: Teachers College Press, 2010.

Anna Maier, Julia Daniel, Jeanne Oakes, and Livia Lam, *Community Schools as an Effective School Improvement Strategy: A Review of the Evidence*. Palo Alto, CA: Learning Policy Institute, 2017. https://learningpolicyinstitute.org/sites/default/files/product-files/Community_Schools_Effective_REPORT.pdf

Brian D. Schultz, *Teaching in the Cracks: Openings and Opportunities for Student-Centered, Action-Focused Curriculum*. New York: Teachers College Press, 2017.

PROPOSAL 17

Weinstein, Gerald, and Mario D. Fantini, eds., *Toward Humanistic Education: A Curriculum of Affect*. New York: Praeger Publishers, 1970. 228 pp.

Focus: A humanistic curriculum designed to "help the student deal in personal terms with the problems of human conduct" and centered around "concerns of all children."

Unique Objective: The preparation of students to engage in "constructive personal and social behavior" and thereby reducing negative social behaviors and societal pathologies.

Program Organization: This proposal for a curriculum of affect links affect with cognition so that the student can learn to cope with his/her own "concerns." It provides a model for developing a curriculum of affect rather that prescribing specific content and instructional procedures.

The model contains several components that are presented in a diagram form to show how the components are related to the whole. These components are specified as follows and are fully described and elaborated in the proposal: (1) Learners, (2) Concerns, (3) Diagnosis, (4) Organizing Ideas, (5) Content Vehicles (multiple), (6) Learning Skills, (7) Teaching Procedures, and (8) Outcome.

Since component two, Concerns, is the unique feature of this proposal, it is the only one here described in detail. (The others are unsurprisingly what one would expect them to be, given their titles, though one should read these sections with care and note how they are linked with one another.)

Identifying Shared and Individual Concerns of students at any age or level of schooling is key to the design of a curriculum of affect for them since these become the foci for organizing the curriculum and for learning to cope with particular concerns held by each student. "Concerns are deeper and more persistent than interests." Three broad categories of concerns are mentioned into which most student concerns may fall: (1) Concerns about self-image/identity, (2) Concerns about disconnectedness/connectedness, and (3) Concerns about control over one's life/power. Whether shared or unique to an individual, identifying the concerns of students is a major component of this proposal and is basic to diagnosing the factors underlying these concerns as clues for selecting appropriate learning objectives and content. Many, many illustrations of possible concerns are given throughout this book, which takes its examples largely from classroom reports from the 1960s Elementary School Teaching Project supported by the Ford Foundation and directed by the authors of this proposal.

Selection of Content: The principal guideline for selecting content given in this proposal is to follow the process inherent in the eight-phase model outlined above. Following the diagnosis of the particular concerns on which learning might focus at any given time (component three), teachers would make judgments about what organizing ideas or themes around which lessons could be designed (component four) would allow these concerns to be addressed. Organizing ideas or themes could be in the form of generalizations, fundamental ideas, principles, or concepts—selected on the basis of the concerns of the learner as well as from academic subject matter. Then in keeping with these themes one or several content vehicles (component five) would be chosen as being appropriate for experiencing the content and reaching the objectives required. Content vehicles may be chosen as they relate to a student's own experience of the personal concerns, feelings about them, or related experiences from the social context. They could be readings, films, videos, projects, exercises, games, or other vehicles. Examples given tend to be projects or exercises in which thought and action are combined.

To convey a sense of what the sequencing of content would look like cumulatively over time, the authors present a "trumpet" diagram on page 164. It provides processes and criteria for attaining personal integration throughout the program.

Teaching Methods and Materials: No novel or unique teaching methods or materials are specified in this proposal. However, more than one hundred pages are given over to providing examples of lesson plans, activities, and methods of evaluation from real school settings that illustrate how to keep consistency across the eight components of the model.

Program Evaluation: This aspect of curriculum development is not addressed explicitly in this proposal. Successful accomplishment of the program's unique objective, as stated above, would seem to be the implied goal and criterion for designing an evaluation of a program of this kind.

Commentaries/Reviews/Critiques:

Terry Borton, *Reach, Touch, and Teach: Student Concerns and Process Education.* New York: McGraw-Hill, 1970.

George Isaac Brown, *Human Teaching for Human Learning: An Introduction to Confluent Education.* New York: The Viking Press, 1971.

John A. Zahorik and Dale L Brubaker, *Toward More Humanistic Instruction.* Dubuque, IA: Wm C. Brown Company Publishers, 1972.

Louis J. Rubin, *Facts and Feelings in the Classroom: Views on the Role of the Emotions in Successful Learning.* New York: The Viking Press, 1974.

Berman, Louise M., and Jessie A. Roderick, eds., *Feeling, Valuing, and the Art of Growing: Insights into the Affective.* Washington, DC: Association for Supervision and Curriculum Development, 1977.

Beane, James A., *Affect in the Curriculum: Toward Democracy, Dignity, and Diversity.* New York: Teachers College Press, 1990.

Mohmmad Khatib, et al., *Journal of Language Teaching and Research,* 4(January, 2013), 45–51.

8

Partial Proposals with a Living Focus

Battelle for Kids, "Framework for 21st Century Learning Definitions," 2019. http://www.battelleforkids.org/networks/p21/frameworks-resources

To master the knowledge, skills, and expertise students need to succeed in work and life in the twenty-first century. Gives a list of key subjects and interdisciplinary themes to be weaved into these subjects (various kinds of literacies), and other outcomes in seven areas: creativity and innovation, critical thinking and problem-solving, communication and collaboration, technology skills, information and media literacy, life and career skills, social and cross-cultural skills. The website also gives a similar framework for Early Childhood Learning and lists exemplary schools and districts that are implementing the model through support of the Battelle for Kids Network and other networks.

* * *

Bremer, John, *A Matrix for Modern Education*. Toronto, ON: McClelland and Stewart Limited, 1975.

To learn how to be a learner through an open, rather than closed, curriculum.

* * *

Federal Security Agency, Office of Education, *Life Adjustment Education for Every Youth*. Washington, DC: US Government Printing Office, 1951. Available at: http://files.eric.ed.gov/fulltext/ED543614.pdf

"To stimulate, fortify, and modify pupil behavior that the school may more effectively promote democracy as a way of life."

Commentaries/Reviews/Critiques:
Harl R. Douglass, ed., *Education for Life Adjustment*. New York: Ronald Press, 1950.
https://www.coursera.org/learn/edref/lecture/9wttA/episode-7-1-life-adjustment-education
William G. Wraga, *American Journal of Education,* 116(February, 2010), 185–210.

* * *

Ontario Department of Education, *Living and Learning*. Toronto, ON: Office of Publications, Ontario Department of Education, 1968

To seek truth through a program of learning experiences in the areas of Communications, Environmental Studies, and Humanities toward the general outcomes of "desirable interests, abilities, skill, attitudes, dispositions, and understandings," "moral development," "physical and mental health," and various personal goals. A big part of this proposed curriculum is individualized with many elective choices. It offers a minimum of structure and grants teachers and pupils wide latitude in formulating choices for each student.

* * *

Rubin, Louis J., ed., *Life Skills in School and Society*. Washington, DC: Association for Supervision and Curriculum Development, 1969

To acquire skills for living, such as "the ability to reason, to adjust oneself in a culture of flux, to control one's time purposefully, to achieve and sustain rewarding relationships with others, and to extend one's uniqueness while participating harmoniously in the society." Related skills identified by contributing authors include: problem-solving, managing one's emotions, becoming a master of one's will and deeds, forming conclusions, making judgments about what is worthwhile in life, the ability to interpret human events in terms of a sound set of values, skills of loving and being loved, and skills of compassion and competence.

Commentaries/Reviews/Critiques:
Stuart Conger, D., et al. *Life Skills*, 3rd ed. Prince Albert, SK: Saskatchewan NewStart, 1971.

* * *

Rugg, Harold, *American Life and the School Curriculum: Next Steps Toward Schools of Living*. Boston, MA: Ginn and Company, 1936.

To provide a curriculum for the upper six grades within a "school of living" that consists of activities of school life, body education, the study of man and his changing society, creative and appreciative arts, work time, the study of the physical and natural world, the study of personality and human behavior, general mathematics, and foreign language.

Part V

PERSON-FOCUSED CURRICULUM PROPOSALS

9

Coherent Proposals with a Person Focus

PROPOSAL 18

Berman, Louise M., *New Priorities in the Curriculum*. Columbus, OH: Charles E. Merrill Publishing Company, 1968. 241 pp.

Focus: The human being as a process-oriented being.

Unique Objective: The development of a process-oriented person in eight broad areas: "a person who has within his personality elements of dynamism, motion, and responsibility which enable him to live as an adequate and a contributing member of the world of which he is a part." Such persons are "ongoing, growing, developing beings." They have "broad rather than narrow or restricted fields of vision." They have internal integrity, are concerned with moral and ethical values, are future-oriented, and have strong skills of judgment and the ability to reconcile conflict. They embrace an education that transcends space, uses time intentionally, allows enough freedom to develop integrity of self-hood, and honors the feeling-thinking cohesion.

Program Organization: The scope of the curriculum is to include eight human processes that should be acquired by the student in increasing degrees depending on the development and maturity of the student. This proposal does not offer a particular way of organizing the curriculum; it does, however, devote an entire chapter to suggesting alternative ways to integrate the eight processes into various curriculum designs.

The eight processes are the following: perceiving, communicating, loving, knowing, decision-making, patterning, creating, and valuing.

The proposal explicitly describes each of these processes including, but going beyond, the common understanding of each of them.

Selection of Content: *Perceiving* is chiefly the process of noticing or attending to stimuli in the environment and categorizing these impressions. (Incidentally, the process of perceiving is discussed in relation to the other seven processes, as is done with all of the eight processes, to enrich the explanations and to emphasize the interrelationships among the processes.

Communicating is the art of sharing personal meaning. This requires interpersonal skills in the use of symbols, language, and various media. "Communication involves a union with one's fellows in which personal integrity and a caring for the other unite to make possible transactions in which one's own meanings become clearer because of mutual concern each for the other."

Loving is the process of relating to other human beings in the attitude of co-responding or with the ability to give and receive "affection, friendship, eros, or charity." To learn the deeper qualities of loving and caring is truly a neglected area in most school curricula. Analysis of the process of co-responding and learning to deal with problems in human relationships are essential components of a process-oriented human being.

Knowing is a process which is usually emphasized in school curriculum to the exclusion of much in the other seven processes. However, an examination and revision to some extent of the conventional understanding of the process of knowing, for inclusion in the curriculum, is encouraged in this proposal. Students need to understand not only the varieties of knowledge that exist but also that ideas are used in additive, systematized, and metamorphosed ways.

The process of *decision-making* is not only one of the most common of processes employed by a human being, but it is also one that requires bringing into play many of our human resources if our decisions and actions are to be of optimum value. Both public and private decisions are complex, necessitating the use of facts and data, the grasp of the relationship between goals and action, the ability to judge matters on their merits, and at a basis level, understanding the personal relationships involved.

Patterning is a process that occurs when we rearrange "concepts, experiences, memories, and plans for future actions." It involves categorizing or ordering things in these various areas. Mathematical patterning is not the only locale of classifying and patterning; it needs to occur in daily life, in our planning, in our emotional life, and in our grasp of new knowledge and understandings.

Creating is the process of "reaching for the unprecedented." The meaning and skills associated with creativity enter into most of human activity, including all the other processes stipulated in this curriculum. Capturing the process of creating, and the learning it entails, are too often missing as a necessary component of schooling.

The eighth process proposed in this curriculum is *valuing*, giving renewed attention to the ethical. The author gives many reasons for addressing this process as an essential feature of learning to be a process-oriented human being. Teaching students to recognize and critique existing values and to create new values may be a difficult task, but it is one that must not be neglected.

In summary, the local teachers and curriculum developers are to fill out the specific content selections in each area for given levels of students within the chosen organizational design of the local curriculum.

Teaching Methods and Materials: This proposal contains several guidelines for teaching each of the eight processes, together with some examples. The usual methods pertinent to each area are expected to be employed by teachers trained to deal with those areas; the book does not contain extensive coverage of these methods.

One special feature in this proposal related to teaching is that it urges teachers to engage in research to learn what methods are successful or not. It offers sample "Hypotheses for Testing" related to the various processes prescribed.

Program Evaluation: Little is stated about this topic except as implied in the discussion of research mentioned above.

Commentaries/Reviews/Critiques:

Louise M Berman and Jessie A. Roderick, *Curriculum: Teaching the What, How, and Why of Living.* Columbus, OH: Charles E. Merrill, 1977.

Leigh Ann Fish, pp. 35–52 in Thomas S. Poetter, ed., *Curriculum Windows: What Curriculum Theorists of the 1960s Can Teach Us About Schools and Society Today.* Charlotte, NC: Information Age Press, 2013.

PROPOSAL 19

Costa, Arthur L., and Rosemarie M. Liebmann, eds., *Envisioning Process as Content: Toward a Renaissance Curriculum.* Thousand Oaks, CA: Corwin Press, 1997. 245 pp.

Focus: A program where the process-content dynamic is taught at three levels (skills, operations, and dispositions) through five states of mind or passions.

Unique Objective: To enable students to confront problematic situations through the use of five habits of mind (The Passion for Efficacy, The Passion for Flexibility, The Passion for Craftspersonship, The Passion for Consciousness, and The Passion for Interdependence), the tools of disciplined choice making.

Program Organization: The authors assert that organizing the curriculum around the traditional disciplines "has dubious merit." They do not, however, want to belittle the place of the disciplines in the curriculum; they call for both disciplinary content and processes to be included throughout the program. The curriculum should be organized around opportunities for students to make decisions related to topics and/or themes. No specific model for organization of the program is provided in this proposal; as long as the program is organized around processes, it will be compatible with the proposal and its purposes.

What is meant by each of the five categories of processes? The Passion for Efficacy is defined as the fact that "humans quest for continuous, lifelong learning, self-empowerment, mastery, and control." The Passion for Flexibility is defined as the fact that "humans perceive from multiple perspectives and endeavor to change, adapt, and expand their repertoire of response patterns." The Passion for Craftspersonship is defined as the fact that "humans yearn to become clearer, more elegant, precise, congruent and integrated." The Passion for Consciousness is defined as the fact that "humans strive to monitor and reflect on their own thoughts and actions." The Passion for Interdependence is defined as the fact that "humans need reciprocity, belonging, and connectedness and are inclined to become one with the larger system and community of which they are a part."

Selection of Content: Individual skills and clusters of skills (operations) are defined in the conventional way in this proposal. (Lists are given on pages 17–19.) Thirteen dispositions, however, are specifically listed as follows with their own definitions (pages 3–13): *Persistence, Decreasing Impulsivity, Listening to Others, Metacognition, Striving for Accuracy and Precision, Questioning and Problem Posing, Drawing on Past Knowledge and Applying It to New Situations, Displaying a Sense of Humor, Cooperative Thinking, Using*

All the Senses, Ingenuity/Originality/Insight/Creativity, Risk Taking, and Wonderment/Inquisitiveness/Curiosity/The Enjoyment of Problem Solving.

These processes are to be woven into and among all themes/decision making opportunities addressed along with appropriate subject matter understandings.

Teaching Methods and Materials: Planning for courses, units, and lessons within the broad structure of processes and dispositions mentioned above is left to teachers and other local educators who may utilize any appropriate teaching methods and materials they choose. There are sections in this book that provide numerous helpful examples of approaches (including assessment procedures) used by teachers in their planning and instruction in schools already following a process curriculum.

Program Evaluation: Little is said on this topic in this proposal. Evidence of student accomplishment of the goals of this kind of process curriculum would certainly be used to evaluate the overall program. Traditional test results would hardly be the kind of evidence required in evaluating this proposal's curriculum.

Commentaries/Reviews/Critiques:

J. Cecil Parker and Louis J. Rubin, *Process as Content: Curriculum Design and the Application of Knowledge.* Chicago, IL: Rand McNally, 1966.

Henry P. Cole, *Process Education: The New Direction for Elementary-Secondary Schools.* Englewood Cliffs, NJ: Educational Technology Publications, 1972.

PROPOSAL 20

Doll, William E., Jr., *A Post-Modern Perspective on Curriculum*. New York: Teachers College Press, 1993. 213 pp.

Focus: Curriculum as a passage of personal transformation

Unique Objectives: This proposal is less specific than many others in terms of its program and content; it is more like a framework for, or a vision of, curriculum. Nevertheless, its purpose is clear and extensively argued. It is based on a rejection of modernist perspectives that dominated much of 20th-century curriculum development and, instead, on embracing more recent postmodern perspectives (an elaboration of which fills much of this book). The purpose is to provide the student with transformative experiences that permit free internal growth rather than mere acquisition of pre-set knowledge.

Program Organization: The author describes curriculum as a process—a process of development, dialogue, inquiry, and transformation. He provides concepts and ideas for generating heuristic curriculum insights upon which local curriculum planners can fill out a program in specific detail. "Filling out a program in detail" may even be too prescriptive a phrase for this curriculum framework since it is meant to be non-pre-set, open-ended, generative, developmental, interactively-derived, and matched to individual student possibilities for transformation of their lives.

Among the features of this sort of curriculum are the following:

(1) **Self-organization:** Students are able to interpret and play with content in imaginative ways; each student internally organizes his or her own learning. Meaning-making is the goal of each student. Curriculum must be rich in multiple perspectives and in diversity, problematics, inquiry, exploration, and heuristics.

(2) **Indeterminacy:** Teachers and students are free, in fact required, to develop their own curriculum interactively with one another; control of the curriculum does not come from external imposition. Questions of goals, plans, procedure, content, methodology, and values are decided within the practicalities of life of the local situation, the student, and the teacher through dialogue.

(3) **Stability across and through Instability:** The process of transformation is open to disruption and reorganization; it is nonlinear. Change is the norm. Challenges, perturbations, disruptions, ambiguities, and mistakes are the sine qua non of the transformative process from which a new equilibrium arises. Order emerges spontaneously out of chaos. "The challenge of an open system is not to bring the process to closure but to direct the transformation in such a manner that the becomingness of the process is maintained."

Four criteria are specified for a curriculum designed to foster a post-modern vision: (1) Richness, (2) Recursion, (3) Relations, and (4) Rigor. Each of these is elaborated thoroughly in the final chapter of the book. Richness refers to "a curriculum's depth, to its layers of meaning, to its multiple possibilities of interpretation." Richness can be developed in any subject through "dialogue, interpretations, hypothesis generation and proving, and pattern playing." Recursion allows "thoughts to loop back on themselves; recursive reflection lies at the heart of transformation." Recursion aims at developing competence—the ability to organize, combine, inquire, use something heuristically." It is not repetition; it is iterative. Relations include both pedagogical relationships and cultural relationships. Rigor in a postmodern perspective involves "deeply felt perceptions and conceptions," looking for "new combinations, interpretations, and patterns," and attempting deliberatively "to ferret out assumptions" and developing "the relation of one idea to another."

Selection of Content: This is accomplished through dialogue with the student and the teacher in the local situation, while adhering to the above concepts and criteria for a postmodern curriculum.

Teaching Methods and Materials: The teacher's role here is one of co-creator and guide. Materials and content may be chosen as needed after goals and purposes are established for students. No specific aids in this regard are given in the proposal. Feedback is especially important in this situation where recursion and lack of pre-determined sequences of learning are the norm. Assessment in the usual sense of testing content is for purposes of advancing student transformation only.

Program Evaluation: It is implied that the goals and purposes of a postmodern curriculum would be met entirely, when the curriculum is evaluated, and that the concepts and criteria specified in this proposal would be found to have been faithfully adhered to.

Commentaries/Reviews/Critiques:

William E. Doll, Jr., *Journal of Curriculum and Supervision,* 8(Summer, 1993), 272–292.

Nancy L. Stuever, *Journal of Teaching and Learning* (No. 1, 2009), 87–90.

William E. Doll, Jr., Slideshow at: http://www.slideshare.net/amandamacintosh79/the-four-rs-final

PROPOSAL 21

Frymier, Jack R., *A School for Tomorrow*. Berkeley, CA: McCutchan Publishing Corporation, 1973. 307 pp.

Frymier, Jack R., *Annehurst Curriculum Classification System: A Practical Way to Individualize Instruction*. West Lafayette, IN: Kappa Delta Pi, 1977. 391 pp.

Focus: Priority is given to the development of the *rationally autonomous individual*.

Unique Objective: Because children differ, there is no one way, no group-oriented way, to present subject matter, to sequence learning activities, or to organize schooling that is best for all children. These educational processes must be oriented toward individual students rather than toward groups of students. An individual's unique life and the living of it must be supported and enhanced by schooling, not destroyed or diminished by it. Thus, a curriculum must be accessible to each individual student that provides the essential ingredients for physical, intellectual, and emotional growth suitable for that individual. (The author presents a series of questions to be answered in attempting to decide the essentials of such a curriculum.) The pieces of the curriculum for a whole school will, therefore, be smaller units than presently provided; they will be selected and arranged in different ways so that different students may have a unique curriculum. Chapter two is devoted to the rationale for honoring the individual student as an end in him/herself (as opposed to subject matter as an end) and for asserting that the rationally autonomous individual is the correct goal of education in the School of Tomorrow.

Program Organization: The essential elements of the overall curriculum to be designed are *actors*, *artifacts*, and *operations*. Actors are those directly involved with an individual's education, such as students, teachers, administrators, and materials and media producers. Artifacts are the ideas or products of human workmanship that represent subject matter or content, such as lessons, textbooks, and films. They become artifacts because of their relationship with actors in the setting. Operations are processes involving modifications over time in actors and artifacts or in their relationships. All three of these elements interact in what is called a *curriculum event*. The task of organizing curriculum is to conceive of innumerable curriculum events or small chunks of curriculum that may be structured individually for each student.

Selection of Content: The following criteria for chunking artifacts are presented: "1) Materials should be in small rather than large pieces, 2) Sequencing and patterning of materials should be as variable as possible, 3) There should be far more stimulus materials than any student could interact with in any given period of time, 4) Materials should be so stored that they are instantaneously available to the teacher or to the learner, 5) Materials should be highly valid, 6) Materials should be varied in form, 7) Materials should be organized and stored in terms of readability, interest, topic, point of view, and the like, and 8) Materials should be available and manipulable for study."

A coding system that assigns a code number to each artifact is to be devised; this implies that a computer system could be used to store and retrieve these artifacts by code number (or some physical system could be devised to provide the same result). A scheme is suggested for coding where figures represent various classifications are established. For example, a code number 145629 might represent an artifact where the first of the six digits refers to a subject matter chunk (say, math) and the second digit refers to a subtopic under it (say, quadratic equations). The third digit might refer to matching low intellectual ability. The fourth to career interest. The fifth to school level (say, middle school years). The sixth to some other characteristic of the content or the student. In a code number like 256730, each digit location would refer to the same classification category as our example 145629, but the number change would refer to a different subcategory within that category. Chapter three discusses the purpose as well as ways to set up this kind of coding system. The goal is to create artifacts for every variable in every category of the classification system. The Annehurst volume (1977) shows how this was done for one school system and displays the entire coding system that was created there.

Teaching Methods and Materials: Students should take a large role in developing objectives, planning and implementing instructional procedures, and performing evaluations. However, sharing these responsibilities with teachers is to be encouraged. An individual student may proceed independently with a curriculum event from the coded system of artifacts once agreed upon by both student and teacher. A group of students might work together on a given coded artifact if all are deemed ready for the same one at the same time. In either situation, teachers should be available to provide normal assistance to learners by initiating whatever professional strategies are deemed necessary (beyond the operations specified in each coded artifact) such that the interaction of actors, artifacts, and operations brings about a successful curriculum event.

A model of instructional decision-making is recommended in this proposal. It includes the following components: (1) assessing the learner's characteristics and the current state of learning regarding the particular artifact, (2) setting of appropriate objectives, (3) selecting a prescription that matches the individual's needs and the objectives at the present juncture, and (4) determining and instituting an instructional treatment. Going through this cycle of four decision points is to be followed for each curriculum event undertaken and should be continued for a second or third round (or more) as required until successful completion of the event is achieved. Details for these instructional and assessment methods are found in Chapters four and five.

Program Evaluation: Mention is made of validation of the Curriculum Classification System in the Annehurst volume (1977), but very little is stated in either volume regarding overall program evaluation. It is implied that success by each student is the ultimate criterion. Individual teachers make the judgment of when a student is ready to go on to a new category of the coded system, but the proposal is virtually silent about how many of these coded categories must be successfully completed in order to fulfill the curriculum at any given level. However, local teachers/curriculum planners are responsible for designing the whole range of the system of curriculum events within the dictates of state requirements.

Commentaries/Reviews/Critiques:
https://kb.osu.edu/dspace/handle/1811/464
James K. Duncan and Jack R. Frymier, *Theory into Practice* (October 1967), 180–199.
"Review of a School for Tomorrow," *Educational Leadership* (November 1973), 180–181.
"A Conversation with Jack Frymier," *Educational Leadership* (April, 1981), 570–572.

PROPOSAL 22

Macdonald, James B., Bernice J. Wolfson, and Esther Zaret, *Reschooling Society: A Conceptual Model*. Washington, DC: Association for Supervision and Curriculum Development, 1973. 39 pp.

Focus: A curriculum that fosters and reflects the "social and cultural values essential for humane development"—"a humanistic-existential personal model of learning."

Unique Objective: To structure the learning environment so that students can explore (expand awareness), structure their experiences into tentative patterns of intellectual and personal relationships (integrate presymbolic and symbolic data), and create personal meaning (transcend these understandings to higher levels of self-esteem, commitment, responsibility, freedom, and action). This proposal is rooted in value choices and in the cultural milieu with its sociocultural, psychological, and transactional dimensions.

Program Organization: The organization of this proposed program can take many forms and would take place in many locations both in and out of school. It would be embodied in areas that lend themselves to student interest and social investigation. Possible structures are suggested, but they would have to be determined in the local situation.

Selection of Content: Skills, knowledge, and commitments are to be learned in operative situations within the holistic-personal contexts of learning environments and not separately or directly taught. These learning environments would include interest centers around common concerns (themes) of our culture that are interdisciplinary in nature. Content is not to be predetermined. It is to be chosen by students in a completely personalized manner that is functionally open in the perceptions and actions of the participants whatever the theme or topics chosen may be. Illustrations are provided, but little direct guidance is given since the content must be chosen in a particular situation. Orientation for this task is found in the overall rationale presented for this curriculum.

Teaching Methods and Materials: Opportunity to accomplish the three-pronged objective of this curriculum (exploring, integrating, transcending) requires the arrangement of the learning environment by the teacher with the requisite resources, student-environment interactions, and ethical commitments appropriate to the themes being addressed. The teacher is a resource, a model of humanistic attitudes and skills, and responds attentively to students as persons. "The teacher does not function as the authority or the final source of knowledge and decision making." Much flexibility is expected of the teacher in determining how to work in this kind of learning environment. Little direct assistance in this regard is given in this proposal.

Program Evaluation: Traditional modes of evaluation are rejected within this model program. Self-evaluation is a natural approach in this type of curriculum. Overall program evaluation issues are discussed, but no specific approach is offered.

Commentaries/Reviews/Critiques:

James B. Macdonald, "The Person in the Curriculum," in Helen F. Robison, ed., *Precedents and Promise in the Field of Curriculum*. New York: Teachers College Press, 1966. Reprinted in *Urban Review*, 8(No. 3, 1975), 191–201.

Norman K. Hamilton and J. Galen Saylor, eds, *Humanizing the Secondary School*. Washington, DC: Association for Supervision and Curriculum Development, 1969.

James B. Macdonald, "A Vision of the Humane School," in J. Galen Saylor and J. L. Smith, eds., *Removing Barriers to Humaneness in the High School*. Washington, DC: Association for Supervision and Curriculum Development, 1971. Reprinted in Bradley J. Macdonald, ed., *Theory as a Prayerful Act: The Collected Essays of James B. Macdonald*. New York: Peter Lang, 1995.

Edwin Mason, *Collaborative Learning*. New York: Schocken Books, 1972.

Virgie Chattopadhyay and Lillian Heil, *Educational Leadership*, 31(April, 1974), 621–623.

John A. Zahorik, Educational Leadership, 33(April, 1976), 487–489.

Richard H. Weller, ed., *Humanistic Education: Visions and Realities*. Berkeley, CA: McCutchan Publishing Corporation, 1977.

Shirley Koeller and Elton Thompson, *Educational Leadership*, 37(May, 1980), 673–675.

James B. Macdonald and David E. Purpel, *Journal of Curriculum and Supervision*, 2(Winter, 1987), 178–192.

Carole G. Basile, *The Good Little School*. Albany, NY: State University of New York Press, 2004.

Ashwani Kumar, *Curriculum as Meditative Inquiry*. New York: Palgrave/Macmillan, 2013.

PROPOSAL 23

Miller, John P., *The Holistic Curriculum*, 2nd ed. Toronto, ON: University of Toronto Press, 2007, 211 pp. (1st ed., 1988, Revised and Expanded Edition, 1996)

Focus: An education of the heart—of the interrelationship of body, mind, and soul

Unique Objective: To align oneself with the basic processes of life which are life-sustaining, organic, and holistic.

This proposal is based on eight principles: (1) a vision that is a lived reality where the parts relate to the whole, (2) there is nothing fixed or rigid about holistic education—it keeps changing, (3) avoid detailed plans but have priorities and a focus on the concept of holistic education, (4) seek change by inner transformation rather than by imposition, (5) accept conflict—it is inherent in existence, (6) see the school as a complex set of interrelationships, (7) acknowledge the nonverbal dimensions of communication among persons so that words take on deeper meaning, and (8) see the school as a living organism, not as a factory.

The idea of holistic education is developed throughout the entire book. The author's vision is stated on the last two pages of the book. It contains the following lines: "At this school we care about kids. We care about their academic work and we want them to see the unity of knowledge. . . . We care about their physical development. . . . We care about how students relate to others and to the community at large. . . . We try to foster their spiritual growth."

Program Organization: There is no preferred organization for the curriculum stated in this proposal. It seems to suggest that whatever curriculum content and design is chosen in the local setting, a holistic vision can be implemented successfully as long as its basic principles are adhered to and appropriate teaching guidelines are followed.

There are chapters devoted to connections that should be maintained to "perennial philosophy," "transpersonal psychology," "interdependent ecological, social, economic, political relationships," and "historical precedents of holistic education," such as progressive education, Waldorf education, and Montessori education.

Other chapters are devoted to intuitive connections, body–mind connections, subject matter connections, community connections, earth connections, and soul connections.

Selection of Content: Generally speaking, holistic education employs transdisciplinary forms of content wherein the integration of nearly all subject matter areas around broad patterns or themes is preferred. Guidelines for content selection are given in this proposal, but no particular curricular content or themes are offered. Decisions are to be made by local educators who know their students well.

Teaching Methods and Materials: The teacher is key in any holistic curriculum. "Teacher as model" or "teaching by example" are basic to working with students toward becoming whole persons. Being able to assist students with integrated learning projects that develop all dimensions of life no doubt requires a teacher prepared differently from traditional teachers who are often trained only in the knowledge or affective dimensions of the curriculum. When infusing holistic education into an already structured program, no matter what the class or teaching assignment the teacher has, there is a need to have competence in the mind, body, and soul aspects of the content being dealt with. Examples from schools operating holistic education programs are provided, but no explicit criteria for how teaching should be conducted are presented. Some special attention is given to how student assessment in this approach should be handled.

Program Evaluation: A few paragraphs discuss "organic accountability."

Commentaries/Reviews/Critiques:

The journal: *Encounter* (Formerly: *Holistic Education Review*)

Scott H. Forbes, http://www.putnampit.com/holistic.html

Ron Miller, *What Are Schools For? Holistic Education in American Culture.* Brandon, VT: Holistic Education Press, 1990.

Anna F. Lemkor, *The Wholeness Principle: Dynamics of Unity within Science, Religion, and Society.* Wheaton, IL: Quest Books, 1995.

John P. Miller, *Education and the Soul: Toward a Spiritual Curriculum.* Albany, NY: State University of New York Press, 2000.

Michelle Kilborn, *Curriculum for Wellness: Reconceptualizing Physical Education.* New York: Peter Lang, 2016.

John P. Miller and Kelli Nigh, eds., *Holistic Education and Embodied Learning.* Charlotte, NC: Information Age Publishing, 2017.

10
Partial Proposals with a Person Focus

Barrow, Robin, *Giving Teaching Back to Teachers: A Critical Introduction to Curriculum Theory*. Totowa, NJ: Barnes and Noble Books, 1984. Chapter 4, Section 7.

To develop physical health, to foster socialization, to educate the mind and coherent reasoning, and to develop moral and emotional maturity.

* * *

Beane, James A., and Richard P. Lipka, *Self-Concept, Self-Esteem, and the Curriculum*. New York: Teachers College Press, 1984

To enhance the student's self-perceptions (self-concept and self-esteem) including the self as member of a family, as a peer, as a person with particular attributes, and as a student.

* * *

Bookwalter, Kevin, "A Theory and Framework for an International Curriculum," pp. 35–50 in Donna Trueit, et al., eds., *The Internationalization of Curriculum Studies*. New York: Peter Lang, 2003

To enable a person to discover, actualize, expand, and refine his/her potentialities and God-given talents. See Curriculum Summary Chart pp. 38–39. This proposal can be implemented in a religious or nonreligious context.

Commentaries/Reviews/Critiques:
The ANISA Model—ERIC ED 110387
Jordon, Daniel C. and Donald T. Streets, "The Anisa Model," *Young Children*, 28(5, 1973), 289–307.

* * *

Cole, Henry C., *Process Education: The New Direction for Elementary-Secondary Schools*. Englewood Cliffs, NJ: Educational Technology Publications, 1972.

To develop those individual skills (perceptual, motor, affective, cognitive, and social interactive) that are essential for acquiring and employing information and experience in making meaning and in functioning effectively in present reality.

Commentaries/Reviews/Critiques:
Harold M. Schroder, Marvin Karlins, and Jacqueline Phares, *Education for Freedom*. New York: John Wiley & Sons, 1973.

* * *

Davis, David C., *Model for a Humanistic Education: The Danish Folk Highschool*. Columbus, OH: Charles E. Merrill Publishing Company, 1971.

To allow a person to become himself. This model began as an open student-driven program for adult education but can be applicable at other levels. It assumes that human beings are "honorable and valuable, prefer peace to violence, love to hate, art to war, cooperation to competition," and can lead their own education.

* * *

Eble, Kenneth E, *A Perfect Education*. New York: Macmillan, 1966.

To promote delight and wonder (a sense of play, discovery, and order); to see the world feelingly (with thinking, knowing, and doing); to foster a life of one's own (with mind, heart, a sense of style and worth).

* * *

Ergas, Oren, *Reconstructing 'Education' through Mindful Attention: Positioning the Mind at the Center of Curriculum and Pedagogy*. New York: Palgrave Macmillan, 2017.

To learn to give active attention to the inner curriculum as well as to the traditional social or outer curriculum. This proposal contrasts the study of the "Me Curriculum" (where attention is not directly in our control) with the "I Curriculum" (where agency and identity are within our control). The education of what one "attends to" is key to this proposal. Reflective and contemplative practices directed to one's mind and inner life are advocated in this exceptionally well-elucidated and well-argued proposal. For a quick summary see pages 296–298 or 316.

* * *

Goodson, Ivor F., Chapter 10, in *Curriculum, Personal Narrative, and the Social Future*. New York: Routledge, 2014.

To acquire personal learning through narrative. Warns against prescribing what is to be learned through the curriculum in favor of narrative learning/ empowerment, and narrative capital.

* * *

Jones, Stephanie M., and Suzanne M. Bouffard, "Social and Emotional Learning in Schools: From Programs to Strategies," *Social Policy Report,* 26(No. 4, 2012), 1–33.

To develop the ability of students to get along with others, regulate their emotions, and successfully manage social dilemmas.
Commentaries/Reviews/Critiques:
Lesley Koplow, *Creating Schools that Heal: Real-Life Solutions*. New York: Teachers College Press, 2002.
Maurice J. Elias, et al., *Phi Delta Kappan,* 98(May, 2017), 64–69.
Nancy Frey, Douglas Fisher, and Dominique Smith, *All Learning is Social and Emotional: Helping Students Develop Essential Skills*. Alexandria, VA: ASCD, 2019.
Joseph L. Mahoney, et al., *Phi Delta Kappan*, 100(December 2018/January 2019), 18–23.

* * *

Kilpatrick, William Heard, "A Reconstructed Theory of the Educative Process," *Teachers College Record,* 32(March, 1931), revised and published as a thirty-page booklet with the same title by Bureau of Publications, Teachers College, Columbia University, 1935

"The curriculum seems best conceived as the succession of educative experience considered with reference to the accumulating educative effect (which) may be thought of either as growing personality or as increasing power and control" by the student.

* * *

Kline, Lloyd W., *Education and the Personal Quest*. Columbus, OH: Charles E. Merrill Publishing Company, 1971.

To prepare students with the linguistic knowledge and understanding associated with our common humanity in four dimensions as defined by the author: (1) Unity, (2) Diversity, (3) Process, and (4) Substance. Emphasis is placed on personal learning with computer-aided resources. A matrix is suggested for covering skills, data, concepts, attitudes, and processes within the four dimensions mentioned above.

* * *

Leonard, George B., *Education and Ecstasy*. New York: Delacorte Press, 1968.

To learn how "to encourage rather than stifle awareness, to educate the emotions, the senses, the so-called autonomic systems, to help people become truly responsive and truly responsible." "To learn delight, not aggression; sharing, not acquisition; uniqueness, not narrow competition."

* * *

Parker, Don H., *Schooling for Individual Excellence*. New York: Thomas Nelson & Sons, 1963.

To provide "a schooling situation in which each child may start where he is and move as fast and as far as his learning rate and capacity will let him." Based on sound psychological laws of learning. Combines training and education in an interactive relationship. Chapters 12 and 13 provide the vision and structure for this proposal. It does not prescribe content.

* * *

Pinar, William F., "Sanity, Madness, and the School." pp. 359–383 in William F. Pinar, ed., *Curriculum Theorizing: The Reconceptualists*. Berkley, CA: McCutchan Publishing Corporation, 1975. "Autobiography and an Architecture of Self," pp. 201–222 in William F. Pinar, *Autobiography, Politics and Sexuality*. New York: Peter Lang, 1994.

To develop the self and one's own identity through a process of self-formation and social reconstruction. The curriculum implied in this model is based on the concept of *currere* and stresses subjectivity and the inner life.
Commentaries/Reviews/Critiques:
Stephen J. Ball, *Foucault as Educator*. Chapter 3. Dordrecht: Springer, 2017.

* * *

Postman, Neil, and Charles Weingartner, *The School Book*. New York: Dell Publishing Company, 1973.

To study and engage in the processes of interactions (relationships) between the individual and other realities, between the individual and various symbol systems, between the individual and culture, between the individual and machines, and between technology and culture.

* * *

Pritzkau, Philo T., *On Education for the Authentic*. Scranton, PA: International Textbook Company, 1971. Also his *Dynamics of Curriculum Improvement*. Englewood Cliffs, NJ: Prentice-Hall, 1959.

To become an authentic human being who has acquired meaningful behaviors through confrontation and dialogue with people and with the disciplines.

* * *

Rogers, Carl R., *Freedom to Learn for the 80's*. Columbus, OH: Charles E. Merrill Publishing Company, 1983.

To facilitate the development of a fully functioning person emphasizing a person-centered way of being and the dignity of the individual. This proposal stresses the importance of personal choice, personal responsibility, and the joy of creativity. The model defines a fully functioning person as one who is free to develop all his/her potentialities; as one who is realistic, self-enhancing, socialized, and appropriate in his behavior; as one who is creative; and as one who is ever changing, ever developing, and always discovering oneself as a person.

* * *

Weiss, Thomas M., Eugene V. Moran, and Eugene Cottle, *Education for Adaptation and Survival*. San Francisco, CA: International Society for General Semantics, 1975.

To challenge students through a humanistic approach to acquire the tools necessary for personal liberation, self-actualization, and cultural survival—the principles, procedures, and ethics of science.

*　*　*

Zhao, Yong, *Reach for Greatness: Personalizable Education for All Children*. Thousand Oaks, CA: Corwin, 2018.

To empower each child to create a distinctive path to greatness by supporting their passions and cultivating their strengths.
    Commentaries/Reviews/Critiques:
Littky, Dennis, *The Big Picture: Education is Everyone's Business*. Alexandria, VA: Association for Supervision and Curriculum Development, 2006.
McDonald, Joseph P., Emily J. Klein, and Meg Riordan, *Going to Scale with New School Designs*. New York: Teachers College Press, 2009.

Part VI

PROBLEM-FOCUSED CURRICULUM PROPOSALS

11

Coherent Proposals with a Problem Focus

PROPOSAL 24

Collins, Allan, *What's Worth Teaching? Rethinking Curriculum in the Age of Technology*. New York: Teachers College Press, 2017. 141 pp.

Focus: "A Passion Curriculum" in which meaningful tasks are the means of acquiring the knowledge and deep skills needed to deal with the complex technological world of today and tomorrow.

Unique Objective: "To develop a community of learners who are working together to address meaningful questions, sharing knowledge, and taking responsibility for completing the challenges they face." Students will develop expertise, share what they learn, develop deep understanding of issues and ideas, make decisions based on evidence/setting/meeting expectations, and utilize the humanities, arts, and social and natural sciences as ways of understanding and affecting the world.

Program Organization: Because this proposal is based largely on the concept of individualized curricula, there are almost no references to how the overall program should be organized. Each student at every stage of the program chooses (with his parent/teacher mentor) what curricular topics to address through projects and investigations. Suggestions for topics are given for students at various stages but only as illustrative and not as prescribed ones or all that might be devised. For instance, at the secondary level, it is suggested that these topics might be focused around career options in categories such as industries or institutions, engineering, economics, government, creativity, or social services. Other problem areas are also possible. Included throughout the book are illustrations from schools having such a curriculum. In this kind of program, local curriculum planners would need to design the overall structure of the program so that all possible options would be available and supported. The idea is to have projects and investigations that are meaningful to students at every stage and level of their studies. While very open-ended in its format, this curriculum would require considerable local planning to arrive at a structure that is feasible and workable.

Selection of Content: With options of many kinds available for student choice, it would seem that content selection would be difficult to specify. However, this proposal has definite recommendations on what should be taught. In fact, the entire book essentially answers this question.

1. In the chapter devoted to Literacy, for instance, the author calls for learning to engage in *dialogue*, to be *persuasive*, and to *negotiate* effectively. Content necessary for this learning to occur can easily be identified for most any topic, project, or investigation.
2. In the chapter devoted to Self-sufficiency, the author calls for learning to be *self-reliant*, to maintain a *healthy lifestyle*, to acquire knowledge and skills *in finance and legal matters*, to *strategic in relation to others* and *self-regulating*, and offers many ideas for content in these areas.
3. In the chapter devoted to Career Skills, the author calls for learning to *think creatively*, to *think critically*, and to *manage time, resources and how to work with others*. The particular skills, strategies, and dispositions required in these areas are illustrated but are left for local educators to fully identify.
4. In the chapter devoted to Public Policy Challenges, the author calls for learning to address *environment issues* (population growth, resources, pollution, species extinction, climate change), *economic issues* (booms and busts, debt, markets, incentives, globalization, growth rates), and *globalization issues*.
5. In the chapter devoted to Mathematical and Scientific Foundations, the author calls for learning various key ideas in mathematics problem-solving *(variables, graphing, functions, use of statistics, correlation, and inference)*, and in scientific problem-solving *(analyzing issues and arguments, various models and theories, identifying research questions and designing investigations, and data analysis and synthesis)*.

Again, these content categories are meant to be illustrative, not author prescribed. And these content areas are to be drawn on in combination as students address their chosen topics, projects, and investigations. They are not intended to be foci for separate courses or instruction.

Teaching Methods and Materials: The role of the teacher in this proposal is that of mentor and resource supporter. A kind of apprenticeship model is recommended for students to follow in this Passion Curriculum. It is explained as occurring in stages: (1) Students come in as novices and work with student mentors who have some expertise on the topic or project of the novice student, (2) They gain experience and work on larger projects with other students, (3) They serve as mentors to other novice students once they have worked on many projects themselves, and (4) They serve as project leaders for other groups once they have become successful mentors. Thus, teaching is seen as a shared role with students taking much of the responsibility. Much of the effort in this kind of shared teaching involves seeing that the required knowledges, skills, and dispositions are embedded in the process of dealing with students' projects and investigations.

As one would expect, the use of technology in this curriculum is discussed throughout.

Program Evaluation: Graduation requirements are discussed and criteria for program evaluation are implied. Otherwise, no formal statements are found on this topic.

Commentaries/Reviews/Critiques:
Joshua Rosenberg and Charles Logan, *Teachers College Record,* October 2, 2017. ID Number 22173.
Allan Collins and Richard Halverson, *Rethinking Education in the Age of Technology: The Digital Revolution and Schooling in America*, 2nd ed. New York: Teachers College Press, 2018.

PROPOSAL 25

Faunce, Roland C., and Nelson L. Bossing, *Developing the Core Curriculum*, 2nd ed. Englewood Cliffs, NJ: Prentice-Hall, 1958. 386 pp.

Vars, Gordon F., and Alice McVetty Vars, Eds., *Core Today! Rationale and Implications*, 3rd ed. Kent, OH: National Association for Core Curriculum, 1985. 14 pp. Available online at: ERIC ED 270376.

Focus: A form of general education that includes experiences thought necessary for all students in order to develop their capacities for effective living in a democratic society. A Core Curriculum is sometimes called A Common Learning Curriculum. It is a form of an Experience Curriculum.

Unique Objective: To acquire knowledge and direct experience in dealing with personal and social issues and problems of common concern to young people and to all persons in a democratic society.

Program Organization: In a program of both general and specialized education where gaining ways of dealing with common problems is central, the usual organization of the curriculum into separate subjects is not considered to be the most appropriate structure for the overall program. Blocks of time and interdisciplinary approaches are typical of *core curriculum* programs.

There are perhaps four or five forms of core organization from which local decision-makers may choose for use within these blocks of time: Type One, based on separate subjects taught by the same teacher to assure that students acquire knowledge and skills necessary for problem-solving (this may not be a true core depending on how it is taught); Type Two, based upon correlation of two or more subjects; Type Three, based on the fusion of two or more subjects; Type Four, based upon common problems, needs, and interests of students within a framework of problem areas; and Type Five, based on teacher-student planned activities without reference to any formal structure. (See chapter 6, in Alberty and Alberty; chapter 8 in Van Til, Vars, and Lounsbury.)

Specialized education may be similarly structured. There may be programs provided for vocational preparation, for the academically gifted, for the handicapped, and for the socially maladjusted. These programs may include elective courses, independent study, ability grouping, multiple tracking, acceleration, seminars, community experiences, advanced placement courses, etc.

The overall curriculum structure may also include required subject matter courses, health and physical activities, personal interest options, and other experiences besides the commonly required core and specialization segments described above.

Selection of Content: Students and teachers cooperatively select problem areas and the personal and social issues on which to focus at every level and time period in the curriculum. The authors indicate that both structured and unstructured content are often chosen for core programs—meaning that in some instances problem categories and issues are predetermined and in others they are not. Several topics and problem areas are listed by the authors as illustrative of what might be used, many of which come from schools that have adopted a core curriculum model. The scope and sequence of core content across all levels of schooling is a difficult matter to monitor, such that both unnecessary duplication and unfortunate omission of appropriate learning experiences are avoided. (See chapter 8 in Alberty and Alberty.)

Teaching Methods and Materials: Core teachers, whether working in blocks of time by themselves or in teams of teachers, choose methods of working cooperatively with students not only in the choice of topics to address but also in how they are addressed. Thus teachers must be quite competent in knowing their students and knowing about social and public issues. They must also be quite knowledgeable about various disciplines and other resources (community resources, for example) so they can be referred to for use as needed in their students' activities and projects.

Unit teaching is often a major approach used in teaching in a core curriculum block-time program. Resource units can be created for future use with topics that arise in a given situation. These will have sample activities, resource information, content references, and lesson approaches, among others, that can be quickly drawn upon when that specific topic is to be addressed. These are usually nongraded since the structure of core is nongraded, but naturally resource units need to match the maturity levels of the students even when similar topics appear at successive levels of schooling. Quite often new resource units will need to be created in situations where topics arise for the first time or where no previously created ones exist. The authors share a number of helpful units in chapter 10 of their proposal. (See also chapter 12 in Van Til, Vars, and Lounsbury, part II of Vars, and chapter 12 of Alberty and Alberty.)

Evaluation of student learning takes on a special meaning in a core program. This topic is fully discussed in chapter 15 of Faunce and Bossing.

Program Evaluation: Chapter 20 in Van Til, Vars, and Lounsbury gives extensive guidance on this topic.

Commentaries/Reviews/Critiques:
William B. Featherstone, *A Functional Curriculum for Youth*. New York: American Book Company, 1950.
Paul T. Dixon, *Clearing House,* 26(February, 1952), 375.
Review of Faunce and Bossing. *Science Education*, 36(December, 1952), 309.

Myrtle D. Toops, *Working in the Core Program in Burris Laboratory School.* Muncie, IN: Ball State Teachers College, 1955. Available as E-Book.

Lurry, Lucile L., and Elsie J. Alberty, *Developing a High School Core Program.* New York: The Macmillan Company, 1957.

Harold B. Alberty, and Elsie J. Alberty, *Reorganizing the High-School Curriculum*, 3rd ed. New York: The Macmillan Company. 1962.

William Van Til, Gordon F. Vars, and John H. Lounsbury, *Modern Education for the Junior High School Years*, 2nd ed. Indianapolis, IN: The Bobbs-Merrill Company, 1967.

Gordon F. Vars, Ed., *Common Learnings: Core and Interdisciplinary Team Approaches.* Scranton, PA: International Textbook Company, 1969.

Curriculum Development Centre, *Core Curriculum for Australian Schools: What It Is and Why It Is Needed.* Canberra, Australia: Curriculum Development Centre, 1980.

Gordon F. Vars, *Journal of Curriculum and Supervision*, 16(Fall, 2000), 70–89.

http://middlegradescurriculum.yolasite.com/resources/Common%20Learning%20Vars.pdf.

PROPOSAL 26

Pearl, Arthur, *The Atrocity of Education*. New York: A New Crisis Press Book, E. P. Dutton & Company, 1972. 365 pp.

Focus: *Education for survival* in a changing world (technological, mass media, complicated social organization, and exploding population)

Unique Objective: "To enable every citizen to exercise autonomy in an interdependent world. . . . *to enable a person to exercise choice.*"

Program Organization: The curriculum is responsible for increasing options for individuals in four areas of life: (1) Choice of a life career, (2) Choice in democratic decision-making, (3) Choice in intellectual matters, and (4) Choice in inter- and intrapersonal relationships. A rationale for each of these areas of the curriculum is fully explained in the context of data presented about knowledge of changes related to these areas and of schooling's failure to address these new circumstances.

Selection of Content: Chapters are devoted to each of these areas of the curriculum. While specific content in each of these areas is not prescribed, there is extensive treatment of topics that need to be addressed and examples of appropriate content are mentioned when referring to existing programs that include these elements. Criteria for content selection, for assuring balance and coherence across the curriculum, and for connecting content to the four goal-areas are included in the descriptive and justifying chapters on each of the four areas of the program.

Teaching Methods and Materials: Some attention to these matters and to student assessment is to be found in this proposal, but there are rarely any unique approaches to teaching offered. A lot of critical attention to poor and inappropriate methods and materials is given while alternative ones (not unusual or unknown ones) are recommended.

Program Evaluation: A form of negotiated program evaluation is suggested but is not discussed at length.

Commentaries/Reviews/Critiques:

Paul Piccone, *Philosophy and Phenomenological Research*, 33(No.1, 1972), 131–133. http://artpearlagainsttheworld.blogspot.com/.

Art Pearl and Tony Knight, *The Urban Review,* 42(Issue 3, 2010), 243–248. https://www.kirkusreviews.com/book-reviews/arthur-pearl/the-atrocity-of-education/.

PROPOSAL 27

Scriven, Michael, "Education for Survival," pp. 166–204 in David E. Purpel and Maurice Belanger, eds., *Curriculum and the Cultural Revolution.* Berkeley, CA: McCutchan Publishing Corporation, 1972.

Focus: Preparation for coping and directing one's life in a volatile society so that one's survival and the survival of the world is attainable.

Unique Objective: To develop the "capacities to *produce*, to *evaluate rationally*, *to relate to*, and *to effectuate*: socially and intellectually revolutionary *suggestions, candidates, threats, and actions*."

This overarching goal would include: (1) "extensive and informed training in discussion of controversial . . . current social issues," as well as the skills and facts for examining and treating social problems, (2) "experiences that make sense out of, give weight to, the many sides of these issues," (3) "spending considerable periods of time with different kinds of people," (4) "effectuation training—working in the field as a constructive change agent," (5) "job skills that will survive sharp shifts in the market's needs," (6) "living skills that transcend one's initial socioeconomic niche," and (7) "life attitudes that do not depend on winning and consuming more than one's peers."

Program Organization: This curriculum would include three major sections: Knowledge, Skills, and Motivation.

The *Knowledge* section would include: (1) Basic facts about the nature of man as an individual, (2) Basic facts about the nonhuman world, (3) Basic facts about the government, economics, anthropology, and sociology of major current and past systems and other, highly deviant ones, (3) Theories of the nature and foundations of government, law, economics, and ethics, and (4) Knowledge for appreciation and reflection.

The *Skills* section would include: (1) The super Rs: speed reading, shorthand/typing, calculating/programming, memory training, analytic reasoning, (2) Interpersonal skills, (3) Scientific method, (4) Creativity, (5) People study, (6) Social (change and survival) skills, (7) Skills of appreciation, (8) Making-crafting, (9) Willpower, and (10) Physical survival skills.

The *Motivation* section would include: (1) Physical (e. g., the desire to exercise), (2) Cognitive (the desire to learn or solve problems, (3) Creative, (4) Moral (the desire to respect the rights of others, to help others), and (5) Perhaps others.

The author gives much attention to explaining and justifying these components of the curriculum. The precise structure a local curriculum would take is left to local educators.

Selection of Content: Guidelines for selecting content are spelled out in this proposal, but specific content within each broad element and component of the curriculum is not prescribed. One guideline urges that content from the disciplines should only be selected to match the requirements of the seven goals listed above; no attempt should be made to teach an entire discipline until post-high school education.

Teaching Methods and Materials: Since there are some very unique purposes and subject matters incorporated into this proposal, some helpful suggestions are provided on this topic within the discussion of each of the elements of the curriculum. However, teachers may need additional help in deciding what approaches to use in many dimensions of the program.

Program Evaluation: A single paragraph is devoted to this topic.

Commentaries/Reviews/Critiques:

Jeannie Oakes and John Rogers, *Learning Power: Organizing for Education and Justice*. New York: Teachers College Press, 2006.

PROPOSAL 28

Sizer, Theodore R., *Horace's Compromise: The Dilemma of the American High School*. Boston, MA: Houghton Mifflin Company, 1984. 257 pp.

Sizer. Theodore R., *Horace's School: Redesigning the American High School*. Boston, MA: Houghton Mifflin Company, 1992. 238 pp.

Sizer, Theodore R., *Horace's Hope: What Works for the American High School*. Boston, MA: Houghton Mifflin Company, 1996. 198 pp.

Sizer, Theodore R., *The New American High School*. San Francisco, CA: Jossey-Bass, 2013. 244 pp.

Focus: The education of intellect and the education of character within a school reform model

Unique Objective: To provide *all* students a personalized academic education in which they learn to use a limited range of essential knowledge to advance their intellectual and character education by exhibiting results from their studies and projects involving the use of a variety of inquiry approaches in solving puzzling questions of a personal and/or social nature.

Program Organization: This proposed curriculum is not designed as a model to be developed and adopted in all settings (except for its broad outline for program structure which is stated below). It is rather a program based on a set of principles that can be developed in many different ways in various settings. The proposal is embedded within a larger school reform effort developed by the author to which all four books cited are devoted. Therefore, a preview about the content of these four books is helpful in gaining an understanding of the context for this proposal.

The 1984 and 1992 volumes are written as fictitious but realistic narratives about a fictitious teacher, Horace, at a fictitious Franklin High School, who converses and deliberates with his colleagues as they attempt to redesign and reform their high school. The result is the set of guiding principles mentioned above and the specific outlines of their new curricular program, together with other changes dealing with teaching, time scheduling, extracurricular activities, and other policy and administrative changes.

The 1996 and 2013 volumes are written in ordinary expository language and describe the work of the author's Coalition for Essential Schools (CES) that based their reform efforts on Sizer's set of nine principles for guiding school reform. The group of schools participating in the Coalition for Essential Schools grew to include elementary, middle schools, as well as high schools (thus making this proposal eligible for inclusion in our book's listing of total curriculum proposals, despite the reference only to high schools in the titles of all four books.). The 1996 volume reports research done on the development and effectiveness of these schools. Both the 1996 and 2013 volumes include commentaries by Sizer on the work of these schools, their struggles, and their achievements. He also extends the discussion given in the earlier books on the beliefs and values behind this proposed reform process.

The primary treatment of the proposed curricular program is found in chapters 8 and 10 and in Appendix B of the 1992 volume. It recommends a program structure of four strands: (1) Communication, Expression, and Inquiry Approaches, (2) Mathematics and Science, (3) The Arts and Literature, and (4) Philosophy and History. For each of these strands there is ample treatment of their definitions and rationales.

Selection of Content: The work of selecting and arranging specific content and activities within each strand for each level of schooling is left to local educators to determine. However, many suggestions on what choices might be appropriate are found throughout the four volumes. Several reports from schools in the Coalition for Essential Education provide further examples and suggestions. One of the nine principles of the CES charges that "less is more" when it comes to content. The so-called coverage of great sweeps of content is replaced with what the proposal defines as "essential content."

Teaching Methods and Materials: Again, helpful suggestions are made on these topics throughout the four volumes. Fictitious Franklin High School, for example, called for quite small class groupings within a schools-within-a-school model, each with its own set of teachers trained in each of the four strands of the curriculum. The teacher in this model is considered to be a coach and students are to be responsible for teaching themselves. The CES principles stress on personalized methods tailored to the needs of students at the appropriate levels of learning and maturity. Also, individualized work should be accompanied by high academic expectations, advancement of strong habits of mind, and regular documentation of mastery. Teachers may draw upon the experience of other teachers in the Coalition of Essential Schools Network in choosing effective materials and methods of teaching.

Program Evaluation: This is touched on only briefly as a curricular task. Evaluation is treated as a part of examining the total reform effort of CES.

Commentaries/Reviews/Critiques: The 1996 volume contains reports of several evaluative studies completed by various organizations.
http://essentialschools.org/about-ces/.
American Institute for Research, *CSRQ Report on School Reform Models*, 2006, Coalition for Essential Schools, pp. 67–74. Online at: http://www.air.org/sites/default/files/downloads/report/MSHS_2006_Report_Final_Full_Version_10-03-06_0.pdf.

Brett Elizabeth Blake and Robert W. Blake, Jr., chapter 15 in Joseph L. DeVitis, ed., *Popular Educational Classics: A Reader*. New York: Peter Lang, 2016.

Deborah Meier and Emily Gasoi, *These Schools Belong to You and Me: Why We Can't Afford to Abandon our Public Schools*. Boston: Beacon Press, 2017. See especially the Appendix.

PROPOSAL 29

Thelen, Herbert A., *Education and the Human Quest: Four Designs for Education.* Chicago, IL: The University of Chicago Press, 1972. 228 pp. (Earlier Edition, Harper & Row, 1960).

Focus: The acquisition and use of three kinds of inquiry.

Unique Objective: To enable students, by means of three kinds of inquiry, to have experiences of what the human being is all about, of what knowledge in the sciences and the humanities is all about, and of what society and its relationships are all about.

Program Organization: In addition to learning basic language and other skills in a Skills Laboratory, the whole of the educational experience must include experience with a combination of three kinds of inquiry: (1) Personal Inquiry, (2) Group Investigation, and (3) Action Research, all three of which all students learn how to conduct.

In the case of Personal Inquiry, each student carries out inquiries to answer self-chosen questions about his/her needs or interests, about his/her own talents and limitations, about relationships with others and the nature of the human condition. The aim of this part of the curriculum would be to develop personal autonomy.

In the case of the second kind of inquiry, Group Investigation, each student participates in inquiry with other people to find out answers to questions arising out of that group's real problems and affairs. The aim here would be to develop habits of inquiry and group dynamics appropriate to participation in the activities of any self-directing group that has a common purpose, whether civic, societal, governmental, occupational, or other corporate decision-making setting.

In the case of the third kind of inquiry, Action Research, students learn to make action plans, test them out, reflect on the results, and then adjust their action plans (perhaps following this cycle several times) until they have cause to believe the action is warranted and will succeed. The aim here would be to develop processes of reflective action that can be employed anytime a person or group contemplates taking some action.

Of course, all three of these kinds of inquiry-learning would be adapted to the level of experience students have, gradually becoming more complex in form as they mature in conducting them.

Selection of Content: This proposal does not rigidly specify the content or the sequence of engaging the content in any of the four parts of the program. However, illustrative activities and descriptive cases abound throughout the proposal such that, together with its stated rationale, content selection by local teachers and schools should not be difficult. Within the four-part structure of the program, the author expects local decision makers to be free to select appropriate content and activities.

Teaching Methods and Materials: Again, the proposal provides little prescriptive guidance in this area. Teachers would necessarily determine what teaching methods and materials they deem appropriate. Much student or student group choice in these matters is recommended, however, as a means of their learning the processes of personal, group, or action inquiry. The most challenging aspect of teaching in this kind of a curriculum would be for teachers to be competent in how each of the three kinds of inquiry is conducted if they are not already well versed in them. The book does offer background information in these matters as well as such practical matters as how groups may be constituted.

Program Evaluation: Treatment of this topic is essentially absent in this proposal.

Commentaries/Reviews/Critiques:

Kenneth D. Benne, *American Journal of Education*, 69(Autumn, 1960), 366–370.

Fred T. Wilhelms, *Elementary School Journal*, 62(March, 1962), 332–333.

12
Partial Proposals with a Problem Focus

Ammons, Margaret, "Communications: A Curriculum Focus," pp. 105–122 in Alexander Frazier, ed., *A Curriculum for Children*. Washington, DC: Association for Supervision and Curriculum Development, 1969.

"To be able to make reasoned and wise choices, to acquire the tools which allow such wise choices, to become increasingly independent in learning, to value learning as a means of coping with the world."

* * *

Bowers, C. A., *Cultural Literacy for Freedom: An Existential Perspective on Teaching, Curriculum, and School Policy*. Eugene, OR: Elan Publishers, 1974.

To have students examine the culture and its underlying assumptions in relation to their current experience of the culture so that they may be free to see options and to make reasonable choices in life independent of present cultural views and norms.

* * *

Hopkins, Richard L., *Narrative Schooling: Experiential Learning and the Transformation of American Education*. New York: Teachers College Press, 1994.

"To put the experience of students into play in the process of schooling and to bring the conventional materials of schooling—the subjects, the disciplines, the courses—into alignment with the actual lives of learners." This proposal calls for learning through real-world projects in settings of situational autonomy; open but structured learning by students as active agents; use of deliberation, reflective action, and narrative communication by students; mentoring (rather than direct teaching) by school staff and others, and the valuing of communal sharing of narrative experiences in the process of creating a new cultural life.

* * *

Marsh, David D., Judy B. Codding, and Associates, *The New American High School*. Thousand Oaks, CA: Corwin Press, 1999.

To bring all students through a standard core curriculum to the level of a Certificate of Initial Mastery by the close of the lower division of high school (grade 10) in a state or national standards-driven program. The upper division (grades 11 and 12) would consist of two programs (similarly standards-driven) where students choose one or the other of the following—one, a college prep program, the other, a professional/technical program.

* * *

Miel, Alice, "A Design for Continuous Progress: Elements and Structure," pp. 123–136 in Alexander Frazier, ed., *A Curriculum for Children*. Washington, DC: Association for Supervision and Curriculum Development, 1969.

"To have the opportunity: 1) for acquisition of symbolic tools; 2) for personal exploration, inquiry, experimentation, and creativity; 3) for systematic exploration of organized disciplines; 4) for cooperative inquiry and problem solving; 5) for experiences in managing an environment, giving service, and governing; and 6) for enjoying literature, the arts, and physical recreation."

* * *

Miller, Patrick F., *Dilemmas and Decisions: A Critical Addition to the Curriculum*. Leiden, The Netherlands: Brill|Sense, 2018.

To develop the capacity to recognize and make decisions in situations where real dilemmas exist—that is, where no clear prudent or moral choice can be justified by a rational argument alone—and yet where a decision must be made. Examples in many subjects are given.

* * *

Murname, Richard J., and Frank Levy, *Teaching the New Basic Skills: Principles for Educating Children to Thrive in a Changing Economy*. New York: The Free Press, 1996.

To teach those new basic skills students will need in order to succeed in an ever-changing economy: (1) the "hard" skills of basic mathematics, problem solving, and high levels of reading ability, (2) the "soft" skills of being able to work in groups and to make effective oral and written presentations, and (3) the ability to use personal computers and to do word processing. This proposal draws on principles used by business and draws on partnerships with businesses.

* * *

Perkins, David N., *Knowledge as Design*. Hillsdale, NJ: Lawrence Erlbaum Associates, Publishers, 1986.

Offers an approach using invention/design features to structure a program that bridges knowledge to product-making. It emphasizes the use of this model in learning both skills and content and the place of reasoning and argument throughout the curriculum. Knowledge has a tool-like character.

* * *

Raup, R. Bruce, George E. Axtelle, Kenneth D. Benne, and B. Othanel Smith, *The Improvement of Practical Intelligence: The Central Task of Education*. New York: Bureau of Publications, Teachers College, Columbia University, 1962, 1978. (Earlier Editions, 1943, 1949).

To learn the rationale for and the processes and the skills involved in making practical social judgments in a democratic society. The proposal provides extensive analysis and illustrations of these decision-making processes for use in any group situation (including schools), in policymaking forums, and in setting the norms of social conduct.

* * *

Swartwood, Jason David, "Cultivating Practical Wisdom," (Dissertation) University of Minnesota, 2013. Available from ProQuest.com—See a related proposal in James G. Henderson and Rosemary Gornik, *Transformative Curriculum Leadership*, 3rd ed. Upper Saddle River, NJ: Pearson Education, 2007.

To develop skills of practical wisdom. For the 2007 proposal: To foster 3S understanding where the student integrates *S*ubject matter understanding with democratic *S*elf and *S*ocial understanding through multiple forms of problem-solving and inquiry.

Commentaries/Reviews/Critiques:
James King, "Non-Teaching and Its Significance for Education," *Educational Theory*, 26(No. 2, 1976), 223–230.
Elliot W. Eisner, "From Episteme to Phronesis to Artistry in the Study and Improvement of Teaching, *Teaching and Teacher Education*, 18(No. 4, 2002), 375–385.
Barry Schwartz and Kenneth Sharpe, *Practical Wisdom: The Right Way to Do the Right Thing*. New York: Riverside Books, 2010.

* * *

Wassermann, Selma, *Teaching in the Age of Disinformation*. Lanham, MD: Rowman & Littlefield, 2018.

To focus on learning to think; includes eleven thinking operations: observing, comparing, classifying, hypothesizing, searching for assumptions, summarizing, interpreting, making decisions, designing projects and investigations, creating and inventing, and evaluating and assessing. Gives many suggested thinking tasks for each operation.

Part VII

VALUES-FOCUSED CURRICULUM PROPOSALS

13

Coherent Proposals with a Values Focus

PROPOSAL 30

Noddings, Nel, *The Challenge to Care in Schools: An Alternative Approach to Education*, 1st ed. New York: Teachers College Press, 1992. *2nd Edition*, 2005. 190 pp.

Focus: Noncoercive schooling that encourages the growth of competent, caring, loving, and lovable people, a moral focus rather than a focus on academic adequacy
　Unique Objective: Educate *to care for* one's physical health, spirituality, occupational, and recreational life, *to care for* one's intimate others at all stages of their lives, *to care for* acceptable relationships with colleagues, friends, acquaintances, and members of social and civic groups, *to care for* acceptable relationships with non-human life, *to care for* created objects and artifacts, and *to care for* ideas and academics.
　Program Organization: The curriculum is to be organized around six centers of caring which all students are to address: (1) Caring for Self, (2) Caring for the Inner Circle, (3) Caring for Strangers and Distant Others, (4) Caring for Animals, Plants, and the Earth, (5) Caring for the Human-Made World, and (6) Caring for Ideas. Other parts of a student's day would be devoted to curriculum beyond these centers of caring.
　Selection of Content: A chapter is devoted to each of these centers of caring with illustrative concepts and explanations but without prescribing particular content. The curriculum for each center of caring is to be constructed cooperatively with teachers and students.
　Teaching Methods and Materials: These are to be based on responses to questions such as: What do particular students need? What are they likely to

be interested in? What sorts of resources should be available if they choose A, B, or C? What can both teacher and student contribute by way of knowledge and experience about the chosen topic? Whom can we call on in the community to help students evaluate their work? What will be studied before and after this unit? What special capacities do they bring to the topic? How can we plan for inclusive experience as well as experiences that center on particular affiliations? How do we plan for continuity of purpose, of residence, of teachers and students, and of curriculum? How do we show respect for the full range of human capacities by offering a variety of specializations organized around the themes of caring?

Program Evaluation: Not much is stated on this topic. Student self-evaluation is to be encouraged. Community members might assist in program evaluation. For example, a horticulturalist might check on understanding of the plant world and the environment.

Commentaries/Reviews/Critiques:
http://infed.org/mobi/nel-noddings-the-ethics-of-care-and-education/.
https://en.wikipedia.org/wiki/Nel_Noddings.
http://www.newfoundations.com/GALLERY/Noddings.html.
http://www.latrobe.edu.au/education/downloads/martin_p_AJEE_Caring_Martin.pdf
George W. Noblit, Dwight L. Rogers and Brian M. McCadden, *Phi Delta Kappan*, 76(May, 1995), 680–685.
Aaron Schutz, *Educational Theory*, 48(No. 3, 1998), 373–393.
Lynda Stone, chapter 23 in Joseph L. DeVitis, ed*., Popular Educational Classics: A Reader*. New York: Peter Lang, 2016.

PROPOSAL 31

Phenix, Philip H., *Education and the Common Good: A Moral Philosophy of the Curriculum.* New York: Harper & Brothers, 1961. 271 pp.

Focus: A curriculum based on moral grounds for a democracy of worth

Unique Objective: To transform persons "from the life of self-centered desire to that of devoted service to the excellent, and at the same time the creation of a democratic commonwealth established in justice and fraternal regard rather than in expediency."

Program Organization: The proposal calls for a curriculum that deals with the major problems of contemporary civilization in four areas: (1) The use of intellectual standards and reason in the search for truth and in personal, political, and mass communications; (2) The employment of esthetic standards in the arts, manners, work, and recreation; (3) The use of ethical standards in relation to nature, health, sex and family life, social class, race, economic life, political organization, and world responsibility; and (4) The cultivation of the attitude and practice of reverence—sincere devotion to what is supremely worthful.

This proposal is based on the value of the common good, which is highlighted throughout the discussion of all four components of the curriculum. It is also argued that democracy requires this form of education for its citizens. The distinction is made between a democracy of desire and a democracy of worth. The former is one that organizes political life to ensure maximum satisfaction of individual interests and desires and sets everyone's desires in conflict with everyone else's desires without regard to the common good. Education in a democracy of desire simply aims to intensify these desires, indicates possibilities for advancing one's desires, and provides tools for effectively exploiting these possibilities. On the other hand, a democracy of worth centers around devotion or loyalty to the good, the right, the true, and the excellent. It seeks to minimize the amount of injustice caused by self-centeredness. It is primarily other-regarding. It honors and respects things of value instead of craving them. It seeks to discover what is of most worth for the most of its citizens. It employs political methods of reason and compromise in seeking the common good. Education in a democracy of worth, therefore, "follows a value principle, not a principle of want-satisfaction." It teaches common loyalties, moral responsibility, techniques of group process and conflict resolution, and respect for others' rights and concerns. It ever seeks to foster excellence in the truly worthful. As you might suppose, the author of this proposal embraces a democracy of worth rather than one of desire.

Selection of Content: Specific content within the four program areas listed above is not prescribed in detail in this proposal. However, chapters are devoted to explaining possible content and the rationale for selecting it in nearly all sub-sections of the four program areas. For example, in the section on "Ethical Responsibility to the Natural Environment," attention is to be given not only to the history of our use and misuse of natural resources, but also to the sciences of nature and of man in order to understand their interrelationship and the consequences of nonethical uses of nature. Even the political issues in controlling population growth are to be included among many other things mentioned. Other aspects of the curriculum are also discussed thoroughly as well as giving guidelines for what can be included. Obviously, local decision-makers would have to make final choices of content.

Teaching Methods and Materials: There is little guidance provided on this topic. The author does say that teachers need to be people who embody the values of intellectual, esthetic, ethical, and reverent responsibility, or students will find it difficult to reach the goals of this curriculum and of participation in a democracy of worth. Some suggestions, however, are provided throughout the discussion of the four program areas.

Program Evaluation: This topic is not addressed.

Commentaries/Reviews/Critiques:

http://www.tc.columbia.edu/academic/o&ldept/cg/cgreviews.asp

F. Champion Ward, *Ethics,* 72(4, 1962), 301–302.

Marty Martin, *Education, Religion, and the Common Good*. San Francisco: Jossey-Bass, 2009.

PROPOSAL 32

Purpel, David E., *The Moral & Spiritual Crisis in Education: A Curriculum for Justice and Compassion in Education.* Granby, MA: Bergin & Garvey Publishers, 1989. 175 pp.

Purpel, David E., and William M. McLaurin, Jr., *Reflections on the Moral & Spiritual Crisis in Education.* New York: Peter Lang, 2004. 298 pp. (Contains full text of 1989 edition plus five additional chapters of reflections on it.)

Focus: A curriculum based on moral and spiritual values and principles.

Unique Objectives: In addition to learning to be "critical, skeptical, wary, precise, and thoughtful," students should obtain skill in the creative and imaginative arts that can provide "richer, truer, more satisfying schema, models, visions, and paradigms" of ultimate meaning that can deal with questions of "where did we come from, who are we, and where are we going." It should draw on our rich political, moral, intellectual, and religious heritage. Students should learn to make sound affirmations and to act on them, while respecting persons whose affirmations differ from their own. Schools need to be transformative places of joy, justice, love, and compassion.

Program Organization: This proposal does not prescribe a particular program of studies; it leaves this to local decision-makers. However, the proposal offers a broad framework of principles, priorities, and orientations. Key components of a program based on the above unique objects would include: "1) An examination and contemplation of the awe, wonder, and mystery of the universe, 2) The cultivation and nourishment of the processes of meaning making, 3) The cultivation and nourishment of the concept of the oneness of nature and humanity, with the concurrent responsibility to strive for harmony, peace, and justice, 4) The cultivation, nourishment, and development of a cultural mythos that builds on a faith in the human capacity to participate in the creation of a world of justice, compassion, caring, love, and joy, 5) The cultivation, nourishment, and development of the ideals of community, compassion, and interdependence within the traditions of democratic principles, and 6) The cultivation, nourishment, and development of attitudes of outrage and responsibility in the face of injustice and oppression." The author provides concepts related to each of these six program elements to assist those responsible for structuring a curriculum based on these ideas.

Selection of Content: Whatever subject matter is chosen must address the goals, sacred aspirations, and moral commitments of the proposed program and its stated rationale. The following criteria "should permeate the entire spectrum of activities—hidden, overt, planned, implicit, or otherwise": (1) Must contribute to *liberation/empowerment/praxis*; (2) Must include *processes, modes of inquiry, theories of evidence and of truth* that help us know and come to accept what we know; (3) Must encompass a *critical consciousness of history*; (4) Must allow for acquiring the *social, democratic, and critical skills* necessary for participation in a viable social community; (5) Must contribute to the individual's *personal joy and fulfillment*; (6) Must embrace *creativity, play, and imagination* that enable us to give moral and religious significance to life.

Teaching Methods and Materials: These are treated only incidentally in the proposal. It is suggested that teachers organize their instruction around key heuristic and critical questions, dilemmas, and problems. Active inquiry and research will best satisfy the student's natural curiosity. It is expected that exceptional knowledge and competence on the part of teachers will be necessary to implement this kind of curriculum.

Program Evaluation: Program evaluation is not discussed.

Commentaries/Reviews/Critiques:

Egan, Kieran, *Curriculum Inquiry,* 20(Spring, 1990), 121–128.

Purpel, David E., *Moral Outrage in Education*. New York: Peter Lang, 1999.

Ross, Sabrina, *Educational Studies*, 40(No. 1, 2006), 101–105.

Shapiro, H. Svi, *Losing Heart: The Moral and Spiritual Miseducation of America's Children*. Mahwah, NJ: Lawrence Erlbaum Associates, 2006.

PROPOSAL 33

Vandenberg, Donald, *Education as a Human Right: A Theory of Curriculum and Pedagogy*. New York: Teachers College Press, 1990. 271 pp.

Focus: An existential, phenomenological, ethical form of general education.

Unique Objective: To become aware of one's obligations and duties to others and to oneself; to know it is right "to keep promises, tell the truth, return services received, repair damages caused, distribute goods on merit, respect people as individuals and not merely use them for our own ends, abide by the rules of equal freedom, refrain from harming others, relieve suffering, and further the development of abilities and humanity in oneself and others"; to learn to make value judgments and moral judgments that will guide one's own conduct; to acknowledge an ethic of human rights in both the explicit and hidden curriculum.

Program Organization: This proposal does not set forth a preferred organization for the curriculum. Goals and objectives of the curriculum are to be infused into whatever content and structure local curriculum planners choose to prescribe. "Human rights and prima facie moral obligations should structure the organization of schooling."

Selection of Content: Knowledge and skills in all areas of a common general education should be available to all students as a human right. While this proposal does not lay out a specific array of content to realize its basic purposes and approach, it does offer considerable assistance on how to make these content choices—first, with respect to the hidden curriculum (the rules by which the school community and classrooms will function) and then with respect to the studies to be pursued through the formal curriculum.

For example, there is to be no denigration of the valuable knowledge in what the author calls the ACTS (arts, crafts, trades, and sports) as over against that knowledge which lies within the traditional disciplines. He gives a strong rationale for claiming equality and value of both kinds of knowledge across the curriculum. The proposal is grounded in a thorough analysis of the epistemology, axiology, ontology, and ethical dimensions of academic philosophy (an excellent tutorial on each of these is presented) and their rightful impact on the selection of content for this proposed curriculum. There is to be solid treatment of *moral education, cognitive education*, and *existential education* throughout the program. The author discusses and critiques several extant curriculum theories (Freire, Hirst, Greene, Spencer, Dewey, Broudy) in an effort to draw upon the best features of all of them consistent with his own theory. He emphasizes the inclusion of both perceptual consciousness and conceptual consciousness in choices of content.

A list of content categories to be dealt with in this proposed curriculum include the following: (1) *the manipulable world*, (2) *the play world*, (3) *the natural world*, (4) *the social world*, (5) *the lived world*, (6) *the world of books*, and (7) *the world of numbers*. These are not meant to suggest divisions of the curriculum but rather the range of areas to be explored in whatever structure the curriculum takes. Each of these is helpfully discussed; content options can readily be inferred therefrom.

Teaching Methods and Materials: These are treated in a limited fashion. However, a full chapter is devoted to pedagogical theories compatible with this proposal.

Program Evaluation: This topic is not explicitly treated.

Commentaries/Reviews/Critiques:

Robert J. Starrett, *Educational Administration Quarterly*, 27(May, 1991), 185–202.

Mark Halstead, *Values in Education and Education in Values*. New York: Routledge, 1995.

Monisha Bajaj, *Human Rights Quarterly*, 33(2011), 481–508.

14

Partial Proposals with a Values Focus

Boyer, Ernest L., *The Basic School: A Community of Learning*. Princeton, NJ: Carnegie Foundation for the Advancement of Teaching, 1995.

To teach preschool and elementary children to become proficient in written and spoken language and in eight "core commonalities" through a coherent curriculum in "a community of learning" characterized by being "a purposeful place, a communicative place, a just place, a disciplined place, a caring place, and a celebrative place." The eight core commonalities are: "1) The Life Cycle, 2) The Use of Symbols, 3) Membership in Groups, 4) A Sense of Time and Space, 5) Response to the Aesthetic, 6) Connections to Nature, 7) Producing and Consuming, and 8) Living with Purpose."

* * *

Egan, Kieran, Annabella I. Cant, and Gillian Judson, eds., *Wonder-Full Education: The Centrality of Wonder in Teaching and Learning across the Curriculum*. New York: Routledge, 2013

To evoke children's wonder in the world about them and in a curriculum that sustains wonder.
Commentaries/Reviews/Critiques:
Cara Furman, *Educational Theory*, 66(No 5, 2016), 666–672.

* * *

Frazier, Alexander, *Values, Curriculum, and the Elementary School*. Boston, MA: Houghton Mifflin Company, 1980.

To focus on a value-oriented curriculum built on values in three primary areas: (1) the world of everyday living, (2) the cultural heritage, and (3) the moral-ethical-political realm. These values would include three pairs of values: accommodation/criticism, appreciation/creation, and allegiance/reform. The suggested structure and content is extensively set forth, albeit for only the elementary school.

* * *

Hantzopoulos, Maria, *Restoring Dignity in Public Schools: Human Rights Education in Action.* New York: Teachers College Press, 2016

To focus education on human rights, wherein the dignity of every student is held uppermost. This program aims to cultivate individual and collective cultures of care, respect, critical questioning, and participation throughout the explicit curriculum, the hidden curriculum, and after graduation. Examples from schools that are embracing human rights education are included.

* * *

Kimball, Solon T., and James E. McClellen, Jr., *Education and the New America.* New York: Random House, 1962. New York: Vintage, 1966; Auckland: Palala Press, 2018.

To learn to make moral commitments in the life of the American public.

* * *

Miller, John P., *Education and the Soul: Toward a Spiritual Curriculum.* Albany, NY: State University of New York, 2000.

To restore a balance to education between the secular and the sacred through attention to soulfulness, contemplation, the arts, and ecology of humanity and the earth.

* * *

Smits, Hans, and Rahat Naqvi, eds., *Framing Peace: Thinking About and Enacting Curriculum of "Radical Hope."* New York: Peter Lang, 2015.
To help young people to understand what they might "long for," to help them recognize their shared humanity and their shared vulnerability, and to apprehend the practice of nonviolence and peace.

* * *

Ulich, Robert, *Crisis and Hope in American Education*. New York: Atherton Press, 1965. 235 pp. Originally published by The Beacon Press, 1951. https://content.taylorfrancis.com/books/download?dac=C2017-0-50646-6&isbn=9780203794357&.

To provide a secondary education that balances quality and equality, social good and individual freedom, unity and diversity. Includes a Common House taken by all students together with a choice among five Houses—House for the Humanists, House for the Scientists, House for the Executive Group, House for the Artisans, and a House for the Workers.

Appendix A: Practical Assistance for Creating a Total Curriculum Program from a Curriculum Proposal

So how do you translate a curriculum proposal into an actual curriculum? There is no simple authoritative way to design a total, coherent curriculum program for a school, a cohort of students, or an individual student. Local circumstances may suggest particular steps that seem suitable for that situation. If you are inexperienced in developing curriculum, Appendix A discusses some useful resources that are available to help guide you through this process. It is almost a short course in curriculum design and development. These resources are well worth studying before undertaking a curriculum design project. For those experienced in developing the curriculum, these resources can serve as reminders of what is known about matters related to program planning.

CHOOSING A VIABLE CURRICULUM PROPOSAL ON WHICH TO BASE AN ACTUAL CURRICULUM

Curriculum analysis requires the ability to determine the extent to which the assumptions underlying the curriculum are valid for the particular class, school, or district. These assumptions consist of their beliefs about the central purposes of education, about the intended audience and the way people learn, about teachers and the best ways to teach, about the subject matter and how it should be organized, and about the community and what it values. Uncovering these sorts of beliefs requires probing beneath the surface of the {curriculum proposal} document, reading between the lines, and making inferences on the basis of scattered evidence.

—George J. Posner, p. 23

The goal is to make fully considered, fair decisions about particular curriculum proposals.

—Decker F. Walker and Jonas F. Soltis, p. 38

To begin with, a choice has to be made among the many options available in the literature (or others similarly created) that propose a coherent curriculum model, such as those cited and summarized in this book. Often the choice is largely a reflection of the beliefs and desires of those who make this choice. However, for the choice to be a wise and defensible one, a thorough analysis of what is actually asserted in alternative proposals should be undertaken before settling on the one preferred and to be made operational.

The fundamental values underlying a curriculum proposal are the first of its many features that should be discerned and assessed in making a choice among which of several possible proposals is considered to be the best for a given situation. Help in recognizing such values can be found in Brighthouse, et al., *Educational Goods* (2018). For a discussion of preferences among values in curriculum proposals, see Berman, "Normative Inquiry: Dimensions and Stances" (1991). *(Note: All references cited in these pages may be found at the end of Appendix A with a brief annotation on their contents.)*

It is also important to look further at the appeal of each proposal in terms of its substance and its persuasiveness. A very helpful guide in doing this kind of analysis is found in Anderson, *Evaluating Curriculum Proposals* (1981). Anderson discusses what makes a proposal persuasive and how to analyze the arguments made on its behalf. Anderson's book includes several analyses of proposals done by the author to illustrate the process.

To analyze not only the arguments made in a proposal but also all aspects of a curriculum plan from its vision and purposes, to its content and organization, to its implementation, and to the evaluation of its strengths and weaknesses, you will find the guidelines in George J. Posner, *Analyzing the Curriculum*, 3rd edition (2004), exceedingly useful. I refer you specifically to several Curriculum Analysis Questions that Posner suggests you might use in analyzing a curriculum proposal (see Table 1.5, pages 20–22). There are four sets of questions here covering a proposal's origins, its assumptions and specifications about its purposes, content, and organization, its use and practicality, and the determination of your judgment about whether to adopt it and implement it. The questions are very practical. The author uses these four sets of curriculum analysis questions to analyze several well-known curriculum models by way of illustration.

Notice that some of Posner's questions address *instructional* planning, methods, and materials (which are not always addressed in proposals that are strictly curricular in nature). These questions may be considered more suitable for developing and analyzing facets of teaching and instructional practice after an overall curriculum model has been chosen and fully developed. While both curricular and instructional features of a program need to be conceived and implemented consistently with each other, the first task is to choose, plan, and adopt a coherent, integrated, and unified model of curriculum and then later proceed to consider plans for bringing it into actuality through appropriate teaching and instructional processes.

Analysis and evaluation of the features of various proposals should not be limited, however, to examining their *desirability* regarding their substance and persuasiveness; it is also necessary to consider their viability and their achievability. *Viability* pertains to whether they can be expected to bring about the desired results over time. Thus, any related empirical evidence that can be mustered that supports the likelihood of obtaining those results should be sought out and taken into account when making choices among alternative proposals—even any evidence of ineffectiveness or of negative side effects (Zhao, 2018). Failing positive evidence, the chances of their succeeding in reaching their goals will remain uncertain and risky. *Achievability* pertains to whether proposals can be expected to be instituted and sustained successfully in the setting or context into which they may be introduced. No matter how desirable and viable a proposal may be, if it is deemed impracticable for it to be adopted and put into operation, it should probably not be chosen.

Walker (2003) has set of guidelines for assessing the substance and justification of a curriculum proposal (p. 78) and a list of fifteen questions to ask regarding its viability and achievability (p. 290).

With the results of your having analyzed a number of proposals that interest you, you will then be in a position to pick the one you find the most appealing and justified for your particular setting and circumstances. You will also be in a good position to defend your choice with various stakeholders who will want to be convinced that it will meet their wishes and concerns.

The normal process by which a justifiable choice among alternative proposals is made is called *deliberation*. This process, ordinarily undertaken by groups of people rather than by individuals, entails making judgments about which elements, which content, which arguments, which overall vision set forth in various proposals best matches the norms, expectations, and circumstances of the setting the group is acting in behalf of. This requires expressing and arguing the pros and cons related to each of the proposals being considered until there is general agreement on which proposal is the best one to follow in their particular situation.

Parenthetically, I must concede that no single curriculum proposal is likely to be appropriate for all students in a given situation. Several different models of curriculum could operate simultaneously in a district, or school, or for different sets of children or youth. The point is that each one chosen needs to meet the criteria of coherence, unity, and defensibility as discussed earlier in this book.

Once a model has been decided upon which has a clear unifying concept and a rationale for its unique purposes and objective, the whole process of designing the practical programmatic aspects of a coherent curriculum will be simplified and can more easily be kept on target. In much curriculum development work, it has been all too easy to specify organizational structures, content, methods of teaching, or other details that are not strictly in keeping with the model chosen. If the parameters of the proposal are constantly kept in mind, this kind of inconsistency can be avoided.

GRASPING THE PLACE OF CURRICULUM WITHIN HISTORICAL AND CONTEXTUAL REALITIES

We need to be able to put new proposals for school improvement into a historical context.

—Elliot W. Eisner, p. v.

Before proceeding with designing a curriculum based on a chosen curriculum proposal, it is always prudent to grasp as fully as possible a truthful and realistic understanding of several contextual factors that impinge upon the decisions that are made in and for the curriculum.

Nothing is more important in establishing a curriculum program than awareness of contemporary realities within which students will pursue their curriculum. While requirements for living life, working, family life, leisure time, or technological capabilities can be projected only imperfectly into the future and may play a rather limited role in making curriculum decisions, *a real understanding of current circumstances of children and youth, of society, of contemporary values and norms, of local and world cultures, of the state of knowledge*, and so on are essential for the decision makers to obtain and to take into account when making judgments about what the curriculum should consist of, whatever model is chosen to be operationalized. It is, therefore, wise to seek out valid research on these topics before proceeding to make program decisions. See Goodlad (1997) and Biesta (2010).

To locate research in some of these particular areas, see, for example, the following suggested sources along with others available in the research literature. For general background on the history of curriculum in the United States, see Rugg (1936), Doll and Gough (2002), Kliebard (2004), Franklin and Johnson (2008), and Null (2008). For an examination and consideration of values and norms in curriculum, see Macdonald (1977), Vandenberg (1990), and Berman (1991). For views on educational goals, policies, and curricula from around the world, see Reimers and Chung (2016). For an understanding of the place of education in a democratic society, see Henderson and Kesson (2004), Noddings (2013), and Feinberg (2017).

For an understanding of the potentialities and capabilities of children and youth who are to be educated, see studies like the ones Robinson (2009) points to and other similar research. For a realistic understanding of contemporary social institutions and their impact on the curriculum, including both their positive features (e.g., swift communication technologies, organized opportunities for human flourishing, and freedom of thought and action) and their possible negative features (e.g., potential economic and social inequalities, cognitive and material oppression through punitive abuse of power, and death and destruction through crime and war), see Massey (2016), National Equity Project (n.d.), and Giroux (2014). Wortham (2011) discusses research on youth cultures and their impact on learning.

Some important contemporary societal and educational issues arising out of these societal realities that need to be addressed in curriculum planning are discussed in Hinchey and Konkol (2018), Jacobs (2010), Noddings (2013), Noddings and Brooks (2017), Sleeter and Carmona (2017), and Tienken (2017). For research on factors related to the curriculum development process itself, consult the citations in Short (online, n.d.). For an examination of the current governance and administrative context within which curriculum decisions occur, see Anderson and Cohen (2018). For a review of the difficulties with Common Core Standards, see Tampio (2018). For studies of comprehensive efforts to employ external interventions to integrate curriculum reform, build internal capacity to implement such reform, and to learn from researching such efforts, see Improvement by Design (Cohen, et al., 2014).

Don't overlook the value of noting what earlier curriculum authorities have said would be needed in future curricula (and noticing how many of these suggestions either did not come to pass or are just as relevant today as they were when they were proposed). See the Appendix B in this book.

With these ideas in mind, one can start in on designing the curriculum.

FINDING GUIDANCE ON THE CURRICULUM DESIGN PROCESS ITSELF

> Curriculum design is a statement of the pattern of relationships which exist among the elements of the curriculum as they are used to make one consistent set of decisions about the nature of the curriculum.
>
> —Virgil E. Herrick, p. 37

While having said that there is no one authoritative way to design the programmatic aspects of a curriculum, it is often helpful to consult descriptions of various ways this process has been conceived and put into practice. Rather than starting into the design process without an agreed-upon set of steps or procedures, or doing so with a quickly cooked up idea of how to go about it, some already available guidelines are worth consulting. Robin Barrow (1984) has a useful discussion of curriculum designing; so does Smith, Stanley, and Shores (1957); so does Eisner (2002); so does Marsh and Willis (2007).

Null (2017) describes the deliberative approach to curriculum decision making in contrast to other alternative models. Walker and Soltis (2009) provide a brief overview of procedures for making curriculum within a larger treatment of curricular aims. For an extensive and helpful Checklist for Curriculum Improvement and School Renewal, see Tanner and Tanner (2007, pp. 481–499). Walker (2003), in Part 2 of his text, gives useful guidance on curriculum change and improvement.

I hasten to add that guidance on this process of curriculum design is often confused with guidance on instruction and instructional planning. Such resources as Wiggins and McTighe, *Understanding by Design* (2005); Tomlinson (2017, on differentiation); Meyer, Rose, and Gordon, *Universal Design for Learning* (2014); Murphy, Redding, and Twyman (2016, on personalized learning); Sheninger and Murray (2017), Colby (2017), and Fullan, Quinn, and McEachen (2018, on designing deep learning) focus more on teaching and instruction and not especially on curriculum planning.

ASSURING COHERENCE IN THE CURRICULUM DESIGN AND PROGRAMMATIC FEATURES

> A coherent curriculum is one that holds together as a whole. Its parts are unified and connected by that sense of the whole. It is not simply a collection of disparate parts. Parts are integrated in ways that are visible and explicit. There is a sense of a compelling purpose throughout, and all parts are tied to that purpose.
>
> —James A. Beane, p. 3

Beane (1995) is a helpful guide for assuring coherence in the curriculum. It highlights the norms and ideals to which the particular elements of the program should adhere in order to achieve coherence. There are no infallible procedures for attaining coherence; it is a matter of examining the elements of curriculum as drafted in a program and cutting out features that are in conflict with the ideal of coherence or adding in others that would make it more coherent.

This is not to say that there are no guidelines that should govern the human interactions related to designing and implementing a curriculum. Fullan and Quinn (2016); Fullan, Quinn, and McEachen (2018); and Henderson,

Castner, and Schneider (2018) have well-researched frameworks for making changes in schools that have drawn favor from numerous leaders in education who have followed them. They certainly can be helpful to those engaged in curriculum design and development. After all, this task is not simply an intellectual one. It is also one of bringing human beings together in a process of deliberation, agreement, and action—in this case, for bringing about the best possible curriculum for a school, for a group of students, or for an individual student. See also DuFour (2015) and Cohen, Spillane, and Peurach (2018).

One last comment. When designing a whole curriculum from early schooling through graduation, it is understandably a very big job to assure coherence throughout the entire program. It not only requires planning and structuring for the desired coherence; it also requires monitoring the actual curriculum in operation day by day, year by year, to be sure that the program stays on track and adheres to the model it is meant to embody. This implies appropriate supervision, keeping records, timely communication, and sometimes cross-school and cross-district collaboration. Every student can have a coherent curriculum, but it takes careful planning in both the stage of designing a curriculum and the stages of enacting and monitoring it to assure that such a goal is actually achieved. Best wishes to all who enter into this effort. And forgive yourself if it does not come out ideally perfect in your initial attempts.

REFERENCES FOR APPENDIX A

Anderson, Digby C., *Evaluating Curriculum Proposals: A Critical Guide*. New York: John Wiley & Sons, 1981.

Describes ways to analyze and critique the substantive content of curriculum proposals and to evaluate the persuasiveness of arguments presented in them.

Anderson, Gary L., and Michael Ian Cohen, *The New Democratic Professional in Education: Confronting Markets, Metrics, and Managerialism*. New York: Teachers College Press, 2018.

Explains the shift in educational governance from public service–oriented administration to control by managers who implement bottom-line expectations under laws dominated by those with narrow ideologies rather than the public good. The authors advocate for democratically determined governance and leadership in education.

Barrow, Robin, Chapter 3, "Curriculum Design," in *Giving Teaching Back to Teachers: A Critical Introduction to Curriculum Theory*. Totowa, NJ: Barnes and Noble Books, 1984.

Defines the essential elements of curriculum design that should constitute any curriculum proposal.

Beane, James A., ed., *Toward a Coherent Curriculum*. Alexandria, VA: Association for Supervision and Curriculum Development, 1995.

Makes the case for coherence in curriculum and provides examples of school programs that approach this ideal.

Berman, Louise M., "Normative Inquiry: Dimensions and Stances," pp. 225–241, in Edmund C. Short, ed., *Forms of Curriculum Inquiry*. Albany, NY: State University of New York Press, 1991.

Discusses the place of norms and values in curriculum proposals, plans, and development. Displays an array of such values among which choices need to be made in support of whatever specific programmatic components may be advocated.

Biesta, Gert J. J., *Good Education in an Age of Measurement: Ethics, Politics, Democracy*. New York: Routledge, 2010.

Raises the question of what the purpose of education is and why it is important to discuss this question in our current situation in a democracy.

Brighthouse, Harry, Helen F. Ladd, Susanna Loeb, and Adam Swift, *Educational Goods: Values, Evidence, and Decision-Making*. Chicago: The University of Chicago Press, 2018.

Identifies and analyzes a number of educational values (such as equality, equity, justice, human dignity, democratic values, freedom of thought, a well-rounded education, and many others) that are involved in educational decision-making; discusses the trade-offs among conflicting values that are often required. Presents research evidence and value choices associated with making decisions about school achievement, finance, accountability, and autonomy/parental choice.

Cohen David K., Donald J. Peurach, Joshua L. Glazer, Karen E. Gates, and Simona Goldin, *Improvement by Design: The Promise of Better Schools*. Chicago, IL: The University of Chicago Press, 2014.

Reports studies of attempts to scale up school improvement across many schools by three outside organizations (Success for All, America's Choice, and Accelerated Schools Project) during the 1980s and 1990s; strategies varied but all involved comprehensive interventions in curriculum, instruction, professional assistance to teachers and administrators, and environmental forces.

Cohen, David K., James P. Spillane, and Donald J. Peurach, "The Dilemmas of Educational Reform," *Educational Researcher*, 47(No. 3, 2018), 204–212.

Summarizes what coherence between curriculum and the school system entails; outlines a framework for research on this topic.

Colby, Rose L., *Competency-Based Education: A New Architecture for K–12 Schooling*. Cambridge, MA: Harvard Education Press, 2017.

Provides guidance for and examples of designing competency-based instruction, assessment, and grading.

Doll, William E., Jr., and Noel Gough, eds., *Curriculum Visions*. New York: Peter Lang, 2002.

Traces some historical sources of visions for curriculum and offers critiques of thirteen postmodern visions of curriculum.

DuFour, Richard, *In Praise of American Educators and How They Can Become Even Better*. Bloomington, IN: Solution Tree Press, 2015.

Gives principles for planning of both curriculum and instruction through Professional Learning Communities. Chapter 8 focuses on processes for the development of curriculum.

Eisner, Elliot W., *The Educational Imagination: On the Design and Evaluation of School Programs*, 3rd ed. Upper Saddle River, NJ: Merrill/Prentice Hall, 2002.

Provides guidelines for designing and evaluating school curricula and discusses the use of educational criticism.

Feinberg, Walter, *What is a Public Education and Why We Need It*. New York: Lexington Books, 2017.

Addresses contemporary philosophical issues about the nature of an education for self-development, cultural commitment, and public engagement.

Franklin, Barry M., and Carla C. Johnson, "What the Schools Teach: A Social History of the American Curriculum since 1950," Chapter 23 in F. Michael

Connelly, Ming Fang He, and JoAnn Phillion, eds., *The Sage Handbook of Curriculum and Instruction*. Los Angeles, CA: Sage Publications, 2008.

Discusses the content of major curriculum movements during this period.

Fullan, Michael, and Joanne Quinn, *Coherence: The Right Drivers in Action for Schools, Districts, and Systems*. Thousand Oaks, CA: Corwin, 2016.

Provides a framework for making changes through school leaders that focus direction, cultivate collaborative cultures, deepen learning, and secure accountability.

Fullan, Michael, Joanne Quinn, and Joanne McEachen, *Deep Learning: Engage the World, Change the World*. Thousand Oaks, CA: Corwin, 2018.

Describes a comprehensive strategy for students to actively engage in deep learning through learning partnerships, new learning environments, new pedagogical practices, and leveraging digital skills.

Giroux, Henry A., *The Violence of Organized Forgetting*. San Francisco, CA: City Lights Books, 2014.

Discusses the existence and impact on children and adults of a society of authoritarianism.

Goodlad, John I., *In Praise of Education*. New York: Teachers College Press, 1997.

Addresses issues facing education with clarity and forthrightness. Provides wise counsel on numerous background factors that must be considered in making curriculum proposals for any school renewal efforts.

Henderson, James G., Daniel J. Castner, and Jennifer L. Schneider, *Democratic Curriculum Leadership*. Lanham, MD: Rowman & Littlefield, 2018.

Outlines a fourfold process for solving curriculum problems by critical pragmatic artistry: professional awakening, holistic teaching, generative lead-learning, and participatory evaluating.

Henderson, James G., and Kathleen R. Kesson, *Curriculum Wisdom: Educational Decisions in Democratic Societies*. Upper Saddle River, NJ: Pearson Education, 2004.

Shows how judgments in curriculum decision-making must employ curriculum wisdom; conceptualizes what curriculum wisdom is and how it should be applied in practice; a nontechnical approach to curriculum planning in a democratic society.

Herrick, Virgil E., "Concept of Curriculum Design," in Virgil E. Herrick and Ralph W. Tyler, Eds., *Toward Improved Curriculum Theory*. Chicago, IL: University of Chicago Press, 1950.

Contains the best thinking of mid-20th-century curriculum theorists on the topic of curriculum design.

Hinchey, Patricia H., and Pamela J. Konkol, *Getting to Where We Meant to Be: Working Toward the Educational World We Imagine/d*. Gorham, ME: Myers Education Press, 2018.

Explores a variety of contemporary issues in education and curriculum that need to be resolved by acting to correct faulty underlying assumptions and by making necessary changes in practice.

Jacobs, Heidi H., ed., *Curriculum 21: Essential Education for a Changing World*. Alexandria, VA: Association for Supervision and Curriculum Development, 2010.

Argues for a new 21st-century version of school curriculum and provides perspectives on its development, its content, its assessment, its use of technology, and other related topics.

Kliebard, Herbert M., *The Struggle for the American Curriculum: 1893–1958*, 3rd ed. New York: RoutledgeFalmer, 2004.

Provides historical background and rationales for what has been included in the overall curriculum of American schools during the past one hundred years or more. This source also analyzes reasons for the acceptance and/or rejection of some of the major curriculum proposals put forth or adopted during this period. Contains valuable historical perspectives for those considering new curriculum proposals.

Macdonald, James B., "Value Bases and Issues for Curriculum," in Alex Molnar and John Zahorik, eds., *Curriculum Theory*. Washington, DC: Association for Supervision and Curriculum Development, 1977. Reprinted in Bradley J. Macdonald, ed., *Theory as a Prayerful*

Act: The Collected Essays of James B. Macdonald. New York: Peter Lang, 1995.

Discusses the need to identify the values underlying any curriculum proposal.

Marsh, Colin J., and George Willis, *Curriculum: Alternative Approaches, Ongoing Issues*, 4th ed. Upper Saddle River, NJ: Pearson/Merrill Prentice Hall, 2007.

Has several sections highlighting various practical approaches to conceiving and designing curriculum.

Massey, Garth, *Ways of Social Change: Making Sense of Modern Times*. Los Angeles, CA: Sage Publications, 2016.

Provides a primer on social change, how it works, and how students can learn to deal with it.

Meyer, Anne, David H. Rose, and David Gordon, *Universal Design for Learning: Theory and Practice*. Wakefield, MA: CAST Professional Publishing, 2014. Available online at: http://udltheorypractice.cast.org/login

Gives insights from research on learner differences and examples of how to design and implement Universal Design for Learning at all levels and across subjects.

Murphy, Marilyn, Sam Redding, and Janet S. Twyman, eds., *Handbook on Personalized Learning for States, Districts, and Schools*. Charlotte, NC: Information Age Publishing, 2016.

Discusses numerous features and methods of personalizing learning for students along with action principles for schools, districts, and states.

National Equity Project, n.d., http://nationalequityproject.org/wp-content/uploads/Lens-of-Systemic-Oppression.pdf

Describes the mechanisms of systemic oppression in its many forms.

Noddings, Nel, *Education and Democracy in the 21st Century*. New York: Teachers College Press, 2013.

Deals with a multitude of issues that must be considered when envisioning and implementing any educational program. Among the issues considered are: (1) the role of democratic practices in education, (2) the meaning of equality, (3) the nature of educational aims, goals, and objectives, (4) the place of the liberal arts and the disciplines in the curriculum, (5) the role of various kinds of standards, (6) spiritual education, (7) political education, (8) critical thinking, and (9) what should constitute the three most essential domains of education (Home and Family Life, Civic Life, and Occupational Life). The author presents arguments for certain preferred positions on some of these issues, positions that sometimes run counter to those prevailing in the schools. A thought-provoking guide to proposal-making.

Noddings, Nel, and Laurie Brooks, *Teaching Controversial Issues: The Case for Critical Thinking and Moral Commitment in the Classroom*. New York: Teachers College Press, 2017.

Discusses ten areas within which controversial issues may be explored in the curriculum and illustrates how they may be addressed (authority; critical thinking; religion; race; gender; sports; capitalism and socialism; money, class, and poverty; equality, justice, and freedom; patriotism; and moral commitment).

Null, J. Wesley, *Curriculum: From Theory to Practice*, 2nd ed. Lanham, MD: Rowman & Littlefield, 2017.

Treats five traditions or orientations to curriculum: the systematic, the existentialist, the radical, the pragmatic, and the deliberative. Makes the case for adopting the deliberative.

Null, J. Wesley, "Curriculum Development in Historical Perspective," Chapter 24 in F. Michael Connelly, Ming Fang He, and JoAnn Phillion, eds., *The Sage Handbook of Curriculum and Instruction*. Los Angeles, CA: Sage Publications, 2008.

Presents an historical overview of the process of curriculum development as it was described at various times during the 20th century by leading curriculum authorities.

Posner, George J., *Analyzing the Curriculum,* 3rd ed. New York: McGraw-Hill, 2004.

Offers a rationale and procedures for doing an analysis of curriculum planning documents, their purposes and content, their implementation, and their evaluation; provides example analyses done on several well-known curricula.

Reimers, Fernando M., and Connie K. Chung, eds., *Teaching and Learning for the Twenty-First Century: Educational Goals, Policies, and Curricula from Six Nations*. Cambridge, MA: Harvard Education Press, 2016.

Contains comparative studies of curricula in Singapore, China, Chile, Mexico, India, and the United States with respect to their including (or not) the list of 21st-century knowledge and skills proposed by the National Research Council in its 2012 report, *Education for Life and Work*.

Robinson, Ken, *The Element*. New York: Viking, 2009.

Points to the potential that exists in every person and the role the curriculum plays in either enhancing or thwarting that potential. Many case interviews are reported.

Rugg, Harold, *American Life and the School Curriculum: Next Steps Toward Schools of Living*. Boston, MA: Ginn and Company, 1936.

Gives a detailed review of the history of curriculum in the United States in the context of changes occurring in society.

Sheninger, Eric C., and Thomas C. Murray, *Learning Transformed: 8 Keys to Designing Tomorrow's Schools, Today*. Alexandria, VA: Association for Supervision and Curriculum Development, 2017.

Offers eight practices by which to transform learning.

Short, Edmund C., *Curriculum Inquiry and Related Scholarship: A Searchable Bibliography of Selected Studies*. http://education.ucf.edu/CIRS/

Lists and annotates a collection of research studies related to curriculum planning and implementation. Provides a process for searching among these citations for topics and subtopics of interest to the searcher.

Sleeter, Christine E., and Judith Flores Carmona, *Un-Standardizing Curriculum: Multicultural Teaching in the Standards-Based Classroom*, 2nd ed. New York: Teachers College Press, 2017.

Provides guidelines for planning curriculum and teaching activities for a multicultural educational program. Provides a multitude of illustrations and teacher quotes from two major projects that followed these guidelines.

Smith, B. Othanel, William O. Stanley, and J. Harlan Shores, *Fundamentals of Curriculum Development*, Revised Edition. New York: Harcourt, Brace & World, 1957.

Stresses the cultural embeddedness of the curriculum and sets forth principles and procedures for curriculum development and change.

Tampio, Nicholas, *Common Core: National Education Standards and the Threat to Democracy*. Baltimore, MD: Johns Hopkins University Press, 2018.

Explores the development and impact of various U.S. national subject-area education standards and associated testing practices; argues in favor of local establishment of curricula and assessments rather than national Common Core Standards.

Tanner, Daniel, and Laurel Tanner, "Checklist for Curriculum Improvement and School Renewal," pp. 481–499 in Curriculum Development: Theory and *Practice*, 4th ed. Upper Saddle River, NJ: Pearson Education, 2007.

Lists fifty-eight considerations for evaluating how well curriculum development is being undertaken in local settings, along with checklists for related topics such as school philosophy, school and classroom climate, administrative roles, professional development, and resources for teaching/learning.

Tienken, Christopher H., *Defying Standardization: Creating Curriculum for an Uncertain Future*. Lanham, MD: Rowman & Littlefield, 2017.

Presents a progressive-experimentalist curriculum paradigm that may serve as a compass in creating local, diverse, and un-standardized curricula for the future.

Tomlinson, Carol Ann, *How to Differentiate Instruction in Academically Diverse Classrooms,* 3rd ed. Arlington, VA: ASCD, 2017.

Offers guidelines on how to plan instruction for diverse students and gives many examples from schools that practice differentiation.

Vandenberg, *Donald, Education as a Human Right: A Theory of Curriculum and Pedagogy*. New York: Teachers College Press, 1990.

Illustrates how educational/curriculum theories may be analyzed for their axiological, ontological, epistemological, and ethical assumptions: Spencer, Dewey, Peters, Hirst, Broudy, Freire, and Greene.

Walker, Decker F., *Fundamentals of Curriculum: Passion and Professionalism*, 2nd ed. Mahwah, NJ: Lawrence Erlbaum Associates, 2003.

Treats all aspects of curriculum work from the role of theory to practices involved in curriculum decision-making and improvement.

Walker, Decker F., and Jonas F. Soltis, *Curriculum and Aims*, 5th ed. New York: Teachers College Press, 2009.
Provides a very accessible overview of practical curriculum work that highlights the importance of setting appropriate aims for a curriculum.

Wiggins, Grant, and Jay McTIghe, "The Big Picture: Understanding by Design as Curriculum Framework," Chapter 12 in their *Understanding by Design,* Expanded 2nd ed. Arlington, VA: Association for Supervision and Curriculum Development, 2005.

Presents a set of procedures for backward designing a curriculum, starting with expected results and working backward to defining goals, activities, and content.

Wortham, Stanton, "Youth Cultures and Education," *Review of Research in Education,* Vol. 35, 1–243 (2011).

Reviews research on the interplay between youth cultures, educational practices, and the accounts given by adults and youth to each other.

Zhoa, Yong, *What Works May Hurt: Side Effects in Education*. New York: Teachers College Press, 2018.

Warns against assuming that a given educational program, policy, or practice will work for all children, for all purposes, and in all circumstances—even when research evidence appears to support its implementation. One needs also to know the evidence of any ineffectiveness and of any negative side effects.

Appendix B: References Giving What Earlier Curriculum Authorities Said Would Be Needed in Future Curricula

Ideas go around, are forgotten, and come around again.

—Anonymous

John Dewey, *Democracy and Education*. New York: Macmillan, 1916.
Katherine Camp Mayhew and Anna Camp Edwards, *The Dewey School*. New York: Atherton Press, 1965. Reprinted from the publication by D. Appleton-Century Company, 1936.
Nelson B. Henry, ed., *American Education in the Postwar Period: Curriculum Reconstruction*. Forty-fourth Yearbook of the National Society for the Study of Education, Part I. Chicago, IL: The University of Chicago Press, 1945.
Ernest O. Melby, *Education for Renewed Faith in Freedom*. Columbus, OH: The Ohio State University Press, 1959.
Kimball Wiles and Franklin Patterson, *The High School We Need*. Washington, DC: Association for Supervision and Curriculum Development, 1959.
Jean D. Grambs, et al., *The Junior High School We Need*. Washington, DC: Association for Supervision and Curriculum Development, 1961.
Thomas E. Gatewood and Charles A. Dilg, *The Middle School We Need*. Washington, DC: Association for Supervision and Curriculum Development, 1975.
George Manolakas, *The Elementary School We Need*. Washington, DC: Association for Supervision and Curriculum Development, 1965.
William M. Alexander, ed., *The High School of the Future*. Columbus, OH: Charles E. Merrill Publishing Company, 1968.
Alexander Frazier, ed., *A Curriculum for Children*. Washington, DC: Association for Supervision and Curriculum Development, 1969.
William M. Alexander, J. Galen Saylor, and Emmett L. Williams, *The High School Today and Tomorrow*. Especially Chapter 12. New York: Holt, Reinhart and Winston, Inc., 1971.
J. Galen Saylor, ed., *The School of the Future—Now*. Washington, DC: Association for Supervision and Curriculum Development, 1972.

Elliot W. Eisner, "The Kind of Schools We Need," *Educational Leadership*, 41(October, 1983), 48–55.

Elliot W. Eisner, "The Kind of Schools We Need," *Phi Delta Kappan,* 83(April, 2002), 576–583.

National Education Association, *Schools for the Sixties*. New York: McGraw-Hill, 1963.

Arthur W. Foshay, *Curriculum for the 70s: An Agenda for Invention*. Washington, DC: National Education Association, 1970.

Warren T. Greenleaf and Gary A. Griffin, *Schools for the 70s and Beyond: A Call to Action*. Washington, DC: National Education Association, 1971.

Lois V. Edinger, et al., e ds., *Education in the 80s: Curricular Challenges*, Washington, DC: National Education Association, 1981.

Edgar Faure, et al., *Learning to Be: The World of Education Today and Tomorrow*. Paris: UNESCO, 1972.

Jacques Delors, *Learning: The Treasure Within: Report to UNESCO of the International Commission on Education for the Twenty-First Century*. Paris: UNESCO, 1996.

Cheryl Lemke, *enGauge: 21st Century Skills for 21st Century Learners*. Naperville, IL: North Central Regional Educational Lab, 2003.

National Research Council, James Pellegrino and Margaret Hilton, eds., *Education for Life and Work: Developing Transferable Knowledge and Skills in the 21st Century*. Washington, DC: National Academies Press, 2012.

Marcella L. Kysilka and O. L. Davis, Jr., eds., *Schooling for Tomorrow's America*. Charlotte, NC: Information Age Publishing, 2014.

Luke Reynolds, ed., *Imagine It Better: Visions of What School Might Be*. Portsmouth, NH: Heinemann, 2014.

Linda Darlling-Hammond, Nicky Ramos-Beban, Rebecca Padnos Altamirano, and Maria E. Hyer, *Be the Change: Reinventing School for Student Success*. New York: Teachers College Press, 2016.

Ruby Takanishi, *First Things First! Creating the New American Primary School*. New York: Teachers College Press, 2016.

UNESCO, *Rethinking Education: Towards a Global Common Good?* Paris: UNESCO Publishing, 2016. http://unesdoc.unesco.org/images/0023/002325/232555e.pdf

Dylan Wiliam, *Creating the Schools Our Children Need*. West Palm Beach, FL: Learning Sciences International, 2018. Chapter 10.

Appendix C: How to Use This Book

Plan to utilize this book in the following ways if you are thinking of constructing a complete and coherent curriculum plan, program, or policy based on any one of the curriculum proposals in this book.

1. Gather together a group of people to form a study group to function for an extended period of time.
2. Let them do some research and draft a document stating the problems/limitations they find with the current curriculum in the particular setting or level with which they are dealing.
3. Let them do the same to document new ideas on what the stakeholders in this setting think should be embraced in a curriculum conceived for the future.
4. Charge this study group to browse this book carefully in an effort to identify a small number of curriculum proposals that might have appeal in addressing the matters they have stated in the two documents they have drafted above.
5. Have the study group engage in preliminary discussion of this book's sketches of these few proposals until they have determined which ones they wish to study in depth.
6. Obtain copies of the original published proposals (for all those proposals identified for further study) and of any related references so that everyone in the study group can have access to them.
7. Schedule sufficient time for the study group to become familiar with all of these selected proposals and begin to analyze their strengths and weaknesses with respect to the facts and desires expressed in the two research documents they drafted.

8. Narrow down the proposals to the one or two the group finds most appealing and suitable for their situation and deliberate on which one they believe should be followed in designing their own particular curriculum. If they cannot pick one of these proposals, they will have to create one of their own.
9. Write down in outline form a set of statements (based on the chosen proposal) that defines the overall model and each of its components as the study group envisions its desired and preferred curriculum for their particular educational setting. These statements need to be expressed in practical, realistic, but flexible terms. (See the required list of components and criteria for defining a full proposal given in this book's introduction. These same elements should be stipulated in any curriculum plan, not only in any curriculum proposal.)
10. Recommend this document for approval by the appropriate authorized decision-making body.
11. If and when officially adopted by this body, create another group of people, a curriculum development group, to plan and design a full-fledged overall curriculum document based on the adopted curriculum outline. (They can find assistance for dealing with this task in Appendix A of this book.)
12. Have other work groups take this overall curriculum document and further delineate particular parts, levels, content areas, and so on within the curriculum, and consistent with it, until all aspects of the program have been spelled out.
13. Set a date when the new curriculum is to be inaugurated and implementation begun. Allow plenty of time for teachers, students, and others to become oriented to the new curriculum and to participate in instructional planning before this date arrives.
14. Proceed with normal steps in supporting, overseeing, and evaluating the new curriculum after its inauguration.

All these steps are no doubt necessary. Skipping any one of them or rushing the process is not likely to yield good results.

About the Author

Edmund C. Short is Professor Emeritus of Education, The Pennsylvania State University, and currently Graduate Faculty Scholar, College of Community Innovation and Education, University of Central Florida. He received his Ed. D. Degree from Teachers College, Columbia University, and has held faculty positions at Ball State University, University of Toledo, The Pennsylvania State University, Georgia Southern University, and University of Central Florida. His academic and professional activities have focused primarily on development, research, and theory in the field of curriculum practice. He has written numerous articles on these subjects in leading journals, handbooks, and encyclopedias. His most widely known books include *Forms of Curriculum Inquiry* and *Leaders in Curriculum Studies: Intellectual Self-Portraits*. He may be contacted at: edmund.short@ucf.edu

www.ingramcontent.com/pod-product-compliance
Lightning Source LLC
Chambersburg PA
CBHW030140240426
43672CB00005B/211